GENESIS FINANCIAL WORKBOOK

GENESIS FINANCIAL WORKBOOK

Chad Durniak

ELM HILL

A Division of
HarperCollins Christian Publishing

www.elmhillbooks.com

Genesis Financial Workbook

Published in Nashville, Tennessee, by Elm Hill, an imprint of Thomas Nelson. Elm Hill and Thomas Nelson are registered trademarks of HarperCollins Christian Publishing, Inc.

Elm Hill titles may be purchased in bulk for educational, business, fund-raising, or sales promotional use. For information, please e-mail SpecialMarkets@ThomasNelson.com.

Library of Congress Cataloging-in-Publication Data

ISBN 978-1-595541222
ISBN 978-1-595541239 (eBook)

A message from me to you...

You may feel and believe you have no hope, no future, and no way out of your current financial situation. But what if I told you that hope can be found, a future can be built, and a way out of your current financial mess can be paved? Would you believe me? I know it's hard to see any light at the end of the tunnel but, trust me, it's there.

You can trust me because God is a master at bringing order to chaos. We see this in Genesis 1 where He spoke creation into a dark formless void. God worked in chaos to bring about something beautiful. He wants to do this with you.

Genesis Financial is the beginning step to bring financial order from your financial chaos by providing a path forward and a way out. It was designed to provide you the truth about money according to God and a simple financial plan that you can easily follow. With simple goals and a step-by-step process, you will begin to see hope return to your finances.

But this does not come without considerable effort on your part. I know from years of counseling individuals and couples in their finances that many will underestimate what is required of them. They usually start off strong but begin to fade after a few months. Soon, they are right back to where they were before we started. As a result of this, I have learned that there are some keys to the success of you starting and finishing this plan but the one that is crucial is *desperation*.

Are *you* desperate? Has everything else you tried failed? I have learned that, when people have their backs up against a wall, they are willing to do things that others are unwilling to do. They are willing to makes changes that they once thought were crazy. People who are desperate are hungry for the truth because they have been fed too many lies and "easy ways out" that led to bigger problems. They realize that what they are doing isn't working and they are willing to follow a new plan regardless of what their friends, family, and neighbors think. ***So, are you desperate?***

If you're desperate and ready to walk a new path
with your money, then you are ready to begin.

The Genesis Financial Process

- The initial meeting is a chance for you to meet your Financial Coach. Your Financial Coach will meet with you regularly to guide you through the process, teach you simple biblical financial principals, answer your financial questions and encourage you along the way. After learning about the program and the Genesis Financial Workbook, you will need to decide if you are willing to commit to the plan and move forward to the workbook.

The Genesis Financial Workbook - Weeks 2-10

- **Section 1: Me, Myself and God's Money**
  - Here, you will work through the first three chapters of the workbook learning foundational spiritual concepts that affect our understanding of God and money, our overall financial condition and how we make financial decisions.
- **Section 2: Steps to Financial Stability**
  - Along with your Financial Coach, the Steps to Financial Stability will walk you through a slow and steady process towards building a simple and easy to use financial plan that honors God
- **Section 3: The Road Ahead**
  - The Road Ahead gives practical financial wisdom that will set you up for financial success in the near and long term.

Monthly Review Meetings - Monthly

- When the Genesis Financial Workbook has been completed, the relationship between you and your Financial Coach continues through regular monthly meetings. These meetings serve as an opportunity to review progress, address challenges and set future goals. Along with the financial coaching comes prayer, encouragement and spiritual support.

Homework

The Genesis Financial Program includes regular homework that is assigned by the Financial Coach according to the schedule set forth in the Workbook. Each assignment will be thoroughly explained and your Financial Coach is available to answer any of your questions between meetings or classes. It is your responsibility to complete each homework assignment completely by the due date set by your Financial Coach.

Our Commitment

You are about to embark on a journey that will forever change the way you see and manage money. It will be filled with ups and downs but will leave you in a much better spot when finished. You will not do this alone. God is with you. He alone is your provider and source of peace. Nothing can match His love for you. He desires for you to get your finances under control and begin managing them according to a simple plan that He has laid out in the Bible.

God also teaches us that, when we need help, we should seek wisdom and counsel from mature Christians around us — this is especially true when you are experiencing financial problems. Having someone in your corner is crucial for your success. Oftentimes, having someone walk through a financial problem with you is the best way to recover from the financial turmoil you are experiencing. They will have the knowledge and wisdom to guide you and be there to hold you accountable when you make a mistake or lose momentum. I like to call these people Financial Coaches. If you are serious about this journey and you want to turn your financial chaos into something beautiful, then you need a Financial Coach. In fact, this book was written with the hope that everyone going through financial troubles would have a Financial Coach walk alongside of them through the book and regularly follow up with them even after its completion. I would encourage you to seek out your pastor or a trusted friend and see who they might recommend as a suitable Financial Coach. Financial Coaching materials are available for them to guide them as they guide you.

God has committed to you to never leave you nor forsake you. He has given you His written word as the greatest financial plan. Your Financial Coach also has made a commitment to mentor you through this journey, be available to answer questions, and hold you accountable when things get tough. Together, we must all make a commitment to bring order, peace, and a plan back to your finances. Now it's time for you to make a commitment. What are committing to?

Unfortunately, this workbook and your Financial Coach are not free. Everything has a price. Oftentimes, we just look at price as something measured in monetary figures. But the price to this book is much greater than its monetary figure. Your greatest cost along this journey will be paid through what I like to call the 4 Ds. These 4 Ds will be required of you throughout the workbook. They are also keys to success in almost anything you will do. So, it makes sense that even after you complete *Genesis Financial*, the 4 Ds will be required for you to keep the good financial momentum going that we will begin today. Here they are:

1. **Dedication** – A commitment to meet weekly and a willingness to put the time and effort into completing each assignment.

2. **<u>Discipline</u>** – Learning God's way of handling money and then choosing to make it a part of your daily routine.

3. **<u>Desperation</u>** – A willingness to give up the way you think about money and handle your finances in favor of God's truth about money and His way of managing it.

4. **<u>Determination</u>** – A willingness to stick with the plan and not give up when things get tough.

Are you willing to commit to these things? If so, in your own words, write your commitment statement to God and to your Financial Coach.

Participant 1:

To God, I commit to _____

_____

_____

_____

_____

To my Financial Coach, I commit to _____

_____

_____

_____

_____

Participant 2:

To God, I commit to _____

_____

_____

_____

_____

To my Financial Coach, I commit to _____

_____

_____

_____

_____

Personal and Contact Information

Name: _____ DOB: _____

Name: _____ DOB: _____

Address: _____

Phone Number 1: _____ Permission to Text? Yes / No

Phone Number 2: _____ Permission to Text? Yes / No

Email Address 1: _____

Email Address 2: _____

Best time to meet:

	Monday	Tuesday	Wednesday	Thursday	Friday	Saturday	Sunday
Times:	_____	_____	_____	_____	_____	_____	_____

Employment Information

Name of Employer (Person 1): _____

Name of Employer (Person 2): _____

Dependents/Children

1. _____ Age: _____ Lives with you? Y / N

2. _____ Age: _____ Lives with you? Y / N

3. _____ Age: _____ Lives with you? Y / N

4. _____ Age: _____ Lives with you? Y / N

5. _____ Age: _____ Lives with you? Y / N

Government/Social Services/Court Ordered Benefits Received – *Circle the benefit you or a dependent/child receives and the amount of the benefit on a monthly basis.*

1. Social Security $ _____   4. WIC $ _____   7. Child Support $ _____

2. Chip   5. Medical Assistance (Medicaid)

3. SNAP $ _____   6. Alimony $ _____

Initial Financial Assessment

Circle the answer that best describes each question.

1. How would your current financial situation be best described?　　**Orderly | Chaotic**

2. When do you pay your bills?　　**On time | Late**

3. If you had an unexpected bill come up like a car repair or a medical bill, how would you pay for that? (*Can circle more than one*)　　**Borrow | Not pay another bill due | From savings**

4. What is your attitude towards money?　　**Live in the moment | Follow a plan**

5. Are you willing to change the way you spend money, pay bills, and manage your money on a daily basis?

    _____

6. Describe your fears, worries, and concerns about money:

    _____

    _____

    _____

7. Name one goal you want to achieve by the end of this workbook:

    _____

    _____

    _____

Workbook Table of Contents

Part 1: Me, Myself, and God's Money..1

    God's Money — My Role...2

    Stop Being Like "Everyone Else"..4

    What You Need, What You Want, and Everything in Between....................8

Part 2: Steps to Financial Stability...13

    Step 1 – The Genesis Financial Income and Expense Worksheet.............14

    Step 2 – Diagnosis...19

    Step 3 – Go Positive..21

    Step 4 – Build an Emergency Fund..32

    Step 5 – The Genesis Monthly Budget and Budget Schedule..................35

    Step 6 – Keeping Track of Your Finances..50

    Step 7 – Open a Checking Account..54

    Step 8 – Debt: A Simple Plan to Get Out..56

Part 3: The Road Ahead..63

    Red Lights..65

    Yellow Lights..68

    Green Lights...70

Final Thoughts...73

Appendix...75

Additional Resources from Alpha Strategies Group...80

INTRODUCTION

It's not your fault, *kinda...*

They say "money makes the world go around." If that is true, then why are not more people being taught about money? If money is so important, then why isn't money a bigger focus in junior high and high school? If you are taught what a hypotenuse is (which you probably have never used outside of your tenth grade Geometry class), then you should surely be taught how to keep a checkbook, build and use a budget, and create a plan so you don't run out of money next week.

These life skills are simply not being taught. Schools have too many other things they need to teach, and most parents are neither doing a good job of teaching their children about money, nor are they modeling good financial habits. Which brings you to why you are here today — to start a journey down a narrow but very important path that could change the rest of your and your children's lives.

So, let's start by being honest. Some of the financial setbacks you have experienced or experiencing now are not your fault because you have never been taught how to manage money. But let me ask you a few questions: *At what point do you know when your dishes need to be washed? At what point do you know when your car needs gas?* These questions seem to have fairly obvious answers, but what about this question: *At what point do you know you have spent more than your budget allows for groceries?* This question can be a bit more difficult to answer. But when you boil it all down, cleaning the dishes is *your* responsibility, putting gas in the car is *your* responsibility, and so is managing money *your* responsibility. So, while you may have never been formally taught by your alma mater or your parents about managing money properly, at some point you have to say, "Enough is enough, I need to learn how to handle money" because it is your responsibility.

And that's what this workbook is about — learning the truth about money and the right ways to manage it. These can only come from one source — God. God alone has given us the perfect prescription to our financial problems. Unfortunately, too many turn to other secular books, financial experts, or friends and family who know little about God's ways of getting you out of your financial mess and on to a path of financial success. This workbook gives you the basics of God's truth on money and a simple plan that will build a solid foundation for moving forward. It will not address everything, which is why your Financial Coach is an invaluable resource. Your Financial Coach is a Christian who has a desire to walk with you through this process, answer your questions, and pray for you.

You can do this. You are neither too old nor do you lack the ability or smarts. You simply have to say to yourself that where you are right now with your money is not where you want to be six months from now. And if that is going to come true, then real change needs to happen in your life. This workbook will bring all the tools you need to make that change a reality. If you are ready, then it is time to begin your pathway to a better financial future.

PART 1

ME, MYSELF, AND GOD'S MONEY

Make me know Your ways, O LORD;
Teach me Your paths.
Lead me in Your truth and teach me,
For You are the God of my salvation;
For You I wait all the day.

PSALM 25: 4-5 (NASB)

God's Money — My Role

Goal

To understand stewardship and your role as the steward.

Connection Points

1. God owns everything.
2. We are stewards of the things God owns.
3. The Bible explains how we should manage everything God gives us.

ACTION STEP 1:

List three things you are responsible for and leave the fourth spot blank:

1. _____
2. _____
3. _____
4. _____

Being responsible for something is probably not new to you, but did you know that everything you are given responsibility over has been given to you by God? And when God gives you things, He wants you to use and manage them correctly. Why? Well, God actually owns everything.

> *God owns everything and He has given some of what He owns to you to manage and watch over carefully — you are a steward. This makes you responsible for God's stuff.*

"The earth is the LORD's, and all it contains, The world, and those who dwell in it." Psalm 24:1 (NASB)

Since God owns everything you have, doesn't it make sense that He would care about *what* you do with what you have been given?

God does care. In fact, He cares so much that He tells us the things we should and shouldn't do with what we are given. This is called *stewardship*. When we follow what God tells us to do, we are being good stewards. When we don't, then we are not being good stewards. So, how do we know if we are following what God says and being good stewards? Well, God tells us in the Bible. And when it comes to money, God tells us a lot. You will be getting into some of these things later in the workbook. But, for now, the first thing you must understand is that God owns everything and that He has given some of what He owns to you to manage and watch over carefully — you are a *steward*. This makes you responsible for God's stuff. Wow! That's a big responsibility.

ACTION STEP 2:

1. What does God own?

_____

2. What is your responsibility with all the things God has given you?

_____

3. If God owns everything, then what are you?

_____

4. How well are you taking care of the money God has given you?

_____

_____

Concept Review

1. Stewardship

> ### _Keys for Understanding_
> ➢ God owns everything.
> ➢ God entrusts us with some of what He owns, making us a steward.
> ➢ Stewardship is how we care for and use something that belongs to another based on how the owner would want us to care for and use it.
> ➢ Roles of stewardship:
> God = Owner; You and I = Steward; Money and Possessions = Things being stewarded
> ➢ In the Bible, God explains how we should use the resources He has entrusted to us.

Stop Being Like "Everyone Else"

Chapter Preview

Goal

Stop making the same poor financial decisions everyone else is making and commit to following a new path.

Connection Points

1. Stop comparing yourself and what you have to others and what they have.
2. Live within your means.
3. Be content with what you have.
4. Pray for God's help in making wise financial decisions.

ACTION STEP 1:

1. When it comes to your money and possessions, describe how you see yourself:

_____

2. When it comes to money and possessions, how do you see everyone else?

_____

There is a myth you believe about your financial situation and it is this:

- *Everyone else* is doing better than me.
- *Everyone else* has more money than I do.
- *Everyone else* has nice stuff.
- *Everyone else* is doing it.

> *Doing what everyone else is doing and being broke with fancy stuff won't cut it anymore as your financial strategy*

There is a good chance you are making a lot of bad financial decisions based on "everyone else." You look at others and begin making comparisons between yourself and them. You look at where they live versus where you do. You look at what they drive compared to what you drive. You look at what stuff they have and wonder why you don't those stuff. The list of comparison goes on and on to the point where you begin to make every decision based on what everyone else is doing and on what everyone else has. Be careful who you follow and with the comparisons you make.

Most of the people you are following and comparing yourself to don't have the money to buy the stuff they have. They weren't happy with what God had given them, so they decided to borrow money to get the stuff they thought would make them happier. The problem with borrowing to buy stuff is that, for some reason, those people you borrow from always want to be paid back. Not only that, but they want more than what they lent. Now, their inbox and mailbox are filled with monthly bills and past due notices on everything they "own" (it's not really owned because the person who financed it owns it).

It's time to follow a new strategy and a different way of living. Doing what everyone else is doing and being broke with fancy stuff won't cut it anymore as your financial strategy. Be different from everyone else. And, if you want to be someone different, you need to begin thinking differently. Here are a few good first thoughts to consider:

1. **Live within your means** – God has given you income which is different from your neighbor or family member. So, rather than buy the stuff that your neighbor's or family member's income can afford, buy the stuff that your income can afford. Spend what you have rather than what you wish you had. That's living within your means.

2. **Be content** – Being content means being satisfied, happy, and at peace with what you have been given. This means you stop working overtime to afford the latest and greatest thing, or you keep the older car that still runs fine rather than that newer car that looks better than yours. God tells us that we should be content with what we have.

> *"Yet true godliness with contentment is itself great wealth. After all, we brought nothing with us when we came into the world, and we can't take anything with us when we leave it. So if we have enough food and clothing, let us be content. But people who long to be rich fall into temptation and are trapped by many foolish and harmful desires that plunge them into ruin and destruction."* 1 Timothy 6:6-9. (NLT)

So, be happy, satisfied, and at peace with what you have. Your future depends on it.

3. **Pray** – Changing the way you think about money and possessions can be hard. Trying to do it by yourself can be nearly impossible, but nothing is impossible with God. So, why not ask Him to help you? There's no one better or more qualified to help you begin this journey than God.

ACTION STEP 2:

Think of alternatives to each one of the following that apply to you. For example, an alternative to a car would be public transportation or getting a ride from a coworker or friend.

1. Car   Alternative(s): _____
2. Apartment   Alternative(s): _____
3. Home (mortgaged)   Alternative(s): _____
4. Credit Cards   Alternative(s): _____
5. Payday Loans   Alternative(s): _____
6. Check Cashing Services   Alternative(s): _____
7. Rent-to-Own Stores   Alternative(s): _____
8. Living paycheck to paycheck   Alternative(s): _____
9. Cable/Satellite TV   Alternative(s): _____
10. Cigarettes   Alternative(s): _____

ACTION STEP 3:

1. What would you be willing to do and what would you be willing to give up so you would stop worrying about money?

_____

_____

_____

2. What would you sacrifice so that you will no longer worry about how you are going to pay that list of overdue bills? _____

_____

3. Successful people do the things that others are unwilling to do. What are you willing to do that your neighbor isn't? _____

_____

Being someone different can be difficult. It will require you to do things and make decisions that your friends and family will laugh at or think as unwise. But if it results in less sleepless nights worrying about your finances and more money in the bank, then isn't being someone different good? It's time to stop following "everyone else" and admit they don't know where they are going. Be different. Choose a new path to follow. Know what you have is God's and that He wants something better for you.

Concept Review

1. Living within Your Means

> ### *Keys for Understanding*
> ➤ Means = money and financial resources
> ➤ God is our provider.
> ➤ God gives you your means based on His knowledge of what you need.
> ➤ Your means are different from your neighbor's or friend's means, so stop comparing yourself to them.
> ➤ Your goal should be to spend less than what God gives you.
> ➤ Debt is the world's answer to living outside of your means.

2. Contentment

Keys for Understanding
➢ Contentment is believing God has given you all you need to live.

➢ When we are discontent, we say to God, *"You are holding out on me."*

➢ When it comes to money and possessions, it's important to know your needs versus your wants.

➢ Contentment leads to peace.

➢ Those who are discontent and look outside of God for their answer will make irrational decisions and emotional purchases, but in the end will find out that they are never truly at peace or satisfied.

3. Praying

Keys for Understanding
➢ Open, honest, and humble prayer invites God to work in your heart to bring about the changes He desires for you.

➢ Prayer must be an everyday practice.

What You Need, What You Want, and Everything in Between

Goal

Understanding the difference between your needs and wants and how an organized financial plan can help you become a better financial steward.

Connection Points

1. Your money needs to follow a consistent plan.
2. Your financial plan should be prioritized by your needs first then your wants.
3. The things you do with your money should bring glory to God.
4. God has made clear promises to care for our needs when we make Him our priority in life.

ACTION STEP 1:

1. Think ahead to one year from now: Would you rather be in a better spot financially or be in the same spot you are in right now?

   _____

2. List three things you are doing right now to be in a better spot financially one year from now:
   - 1. _____
   - 2. _____
   - 3. _____

Being in a better financial position doesn't come with wishful thinking. It doesn't begin with playing the lottery. It begins with thinking differently and with a plan to match. A plan for your money is you saying to yourself that you are going to follow a set of predetermined steps with whatever income you have. It's you telling your money where to go **before** you get paid, not **after** you get paid.

To do this, you need to decide what your money should do first, second, third, and so on. Essentially, you need to create a list of the **most important** things your money **needs** to do. Please notice that the words "most important" and "needs" are emphasized. That's because many people use their money for the **least important** things, which happen to be the things they **want**.

Building a plan for your money is based on "priorities" and "needs."

- **Priorities** – A list of things from the most important to the least important.
- **Needs** – The things that are necessary to stay alive.

Everyone has needs and these are the things we need in order to stay alive. At the same time, most people have things they want. The things we *want* aren't needs because life wouldn't cease to exist if we didn't have these things. Sure, life might be a bit different and, in some cases, a little more complicated, but life would go on without that extra car, the expanded cable package, and the midday fix at the coffee place or fast food restaurant.

> Our wants have turned into needs because we refuse to deny ourselves of anything.

Part of our problem is that it is too difficult to tell ourselves "no." Our wants have turned into needs because we refuse to deny ourselves of anything. We are really good at telling others they can't have something, but it is a whole lot harder to say no to ourselves. This begins the path down the slippery slope to where everything we spend our money on is a need and every one of these needs is our number one priority. It is absolutely essential for you to begin differentiating between your needs and wants. This will help you build a consistent plan for your money and be in a better financial spot.

ACTION STEP 2:

1. Think about how you spend your money right now and write down a list of where your money goes. Next to it, ask yourself if it is a need or a want (a "want" is something you desire but not necessary for you to stay alive) and circle it. Then, rank how important it is to you on a scale of 1-10 (1 being the least important up to 10 being the most important).

1. _____ Need or Want _____ (1 – 10)
2. _____ Need or Want _____
3. _____ Need or Want _____
4. _____ Need or Want _____
5. _____ Need or Want _____
6. _____ Need or Want _____
7. _____ Need or Want _____
8. _____ Need or Want _____
9. _____ Need or Want _____
10. _____ Need or Want _____
11. _____ Need or Want _____
12. _____ Need or Want _____
13. _____ Need or Want _____
14. _____ Need or Want _____
15. _____ Need or Want _____
16. _____ Need or Want _____

Without a detailed plan that is written out, there is a good chance you will use your money for the least important things before the most important things. In other words, you will buy your wants before your needs. This will satisfy your cravings (wants) and leave you with a temporary "high," but it quickly fades as you run out of money to pay for the more important needs like housing and food. This leads to you feeling like your money is out of control and that you can never get ahead.

Before you move on to building your own plan, stop for a moment and think about what *stewardship* means. If you remember, God has given you some of His money for you to use. Using it for the least important things before taking care of the most important things is not good stewardship. Here is the promise that God makes to you if you know Jesus as your Lord and Savior:

> *"No one can serve two masters. For you will hate one and love the other; you will be devoted to one and despise the other. You cannot serve both God and money.*
>
> *"That is why I tell you not to worry about everyday life—whether you have enough food and drink, or enough clothes to wear. Isn't life more than food, and your body more than clothing? Look at the birds. They don't plant or harvest or store food in barns, for your heavenly Father feeds them. And aren't you far more valuable to him than they are? Can all your worries add a single moment to your life?*
>
> *"And why worry about your clothing? Look at the lilies of the field and how they grow. They don't work or make their clothing, yet Solomon in all his glory was not dressed as beautifully as they are. And if God cares so wonderfully for wildflowers that are here today and thrown into the fire tomorrow, he will certainly care for you. Why do you have so little faith?*
>
> *"So don't worry about these things, saying, 'What will we eat? What will we drink? What will we wear?' These things dominate the thoughts of unbelievers, but your heavenly Father already knows all your needs. Seek the Kingdom of God above all else, and live righteously, and he will give you everything you need."* Matthew 6:24-33 (NLT)

As humans, we are prone to worry and have the wrong priorities. With God's help, we no longer have to worry when we make Jesus our priority. When Jesus becomes the most important thing in your life and you follow what He says, your Father in Heaven will care for you in ways you could never care for yourself, even if you have all the money in the world!

So, when you are creating a list of the **most important** things your money **needs** to do, ask yourself if those things bring honor and glory to God. Are they things He would want you to do with His money? If they are, then there is a good chance you are being a good steward. If not, then ask yourself if you should continue spending your money on that thing or if maybe it should be moved down the list of priorities. And remember, you have a Father in Heaven who knows your needs.

Concept Review

1. Needs, Wants, and Priorities

> ### _Keys for Understanding_
> - **Needs** = The things that are necessary for us to stay alive.
> - **Wants** = The things you may desire but are unnecessary for daily survival.
> - **Priorities** = A list of things from the most important to the least important.
> - Good stewardship, living within your means, and contentment all require you to know your financial needs from your wants and the possessions you need from those you want.
> - A written financial plan will help identify and prioritize your needs.

PART 2

STEPS TO FINANCIAL STABILITY

*"Commit your way to the LORD,
Trust also in Him, and He will do it."*

PSALM 37:5 (NASB)

Step 1:
The Genesis Financial Income and Expense Worksheet

Chapter Preview

Goal

Bring organization to your income and expenses and gain an honest perspective on your current financial situation.

Connection Points

1. Starting a financial plan will help you become a better steward of God's money.
2. The steps to financial stability require commitment throughout the process.
3. The Genesis Financial Income and Expense Worksheet involves gathering accurate and detailed income and expense figures.

So far, "Me, Myself, and God's Money" has taught some very basic truths about stewardship; living differently from everyone else; and understanding the difference between your needs, wants, and what is most important. You have a good foundation and are now ready to move forward into the "Steps to Financial Stability."

The steps to financial stability were created to be simple and easy ways to help you manage God's money every day while building towards a brighter future. It, however, requires something from you — a level of commitment that you may have never made before with money. Committed to what, though? You must commit yourself to completing each step properly and staying disciplined with the decisions you make. Think of it this way — a football player who has the ball has a goal of running to the end zone to score a touchdown. That player, however, must stay in the playing field while he tries to make it to the end zone. How silly would it be if there were no sidelines and players could run wherever they wanted, even into the stands, to accomplish their goal. Sidelines exist for a reason and the shortest way to score a touchdown is a straight line. The steps outlined throughout the workbook are like your playing field complete with sidelines, and the shortest way to reach your goal is to stick to the steps.

Making it this far means you are ready to begin **Step 1 — completing the Genesis Financial Income and Expense Worksheet**. This worksheet forces you to take an honest look at where you are financially and puts you on a path to where you want to be. It will require you to spend a few hours gathering basic information and fill in the blanks. Here is what you will need to complete the worksheet:

- One to three hours of uninterrupted time.
- Monthly dollar amounts from all income sources (jobs, unemployment, alimony, Social Security, child support, etc.)
- All bills and expenses — small, large, old, and new. It doesn't matter whether you think it is significant or not — put it down. Don't forget the little things like coffee, snacks, and lunches.

While the worksheet is simple and easy to complete, it won't work unless you use accurate and complete information. Good results can't come from bad information. So, let's start with the right foot forward.

Action Step 1:

1. Complete the Genesis Financial Income and Expense Worksheet.

Make sure you complete it before the next class or give it to your Financial Coach by a set due date.

Genesis Financial Tip:
Stop Surviving and Start Living!

Before, you were asked if you wanted to be in the same or better financial position one year from now. I know it's hard to think about a year from now when you have so much on your plate right now. Bills, groceries, car problems, and lack of a steady job make you think about just surviving today, so why care about a year from now when you are not even thinking about tomorrow…right? Because tomorrow depends on what you do today, and one year from now depends on what you do tomorrow. If you want to be in a better financial position a year from now, then you need to be willing to start with making changes today to make tomorrow better. Stop surviving and start living!

GENESIS FINANCIAL INCOME AND EXPENSE WORKSHEET

Follow each step to complete the worksheet. Make sure your information is accurate. Don't leave anything out. If you don't have an income source or bill/expense that is listed, just leave it blank. If something isn't listed, use the rows marked "Miscellaneous." Use the average amount for income or expenses that vary from month to month. Make sure all income and expense amounts are monthly.

Income

	Step 1 *List all income sources.*	Step 2 *Fill in the actual monthly after-tax income you receive from all sources.*	Step 3 *Fill in the next three dates you will be paid.*		
		Actual Amount	**Pay Date 1**	**Pay Date 2**	**Pay Date 3**
Wage/Salary 1 _____					
Wage/Salary 2 _____					
Social Security _____					
Unemployment _____					
Child Support _____					
Miscellaneous Income _____					
Total Income					

Expenses

	Step 4 *For every bill or expense, fill in the actual monthly amount you owe.*	Step 5 *Fill in when the bill or expense is due.*	Step 6 *Mark each bill or expense as a need or a want.*	Step 7 *If the bill or expense is overdue place an "X."*	Step 8 *Fill in any past due balance for every bill or expense.*
	Actual Amount	**Due Date**	**Need or Want**	**Overdue?**	**Balance Owed**
Giving, Offerings, and Charities					
Giving 1: _____					
Giving 2: _____					
Giving 3: _____					
Giving 4: _____					
Total Giving					
Paying Yourself					
Investments					
Savings Account					
Emergency Savings Account					
Total Savings					
Living Expenses					
Mortgage/Rent					
Real Estate Tax					
School Tax					
Maintenance					
Other Living Expense _____					
Other Living Expense _____					
Total Living Expenses					
Food					
SNAP (food stamps do not count as expense)					
Groceries					
Dining Out					
Total Food Expenses					

	Actual Amount	Due Date	Need or Want	Overdue?	Balance Owed
Utilities					
Water					
Sewer					
Electric					
Natural Gas					
Cell Phone					
Internet					
Other Utility_____					
Total Utility Expenses					
Transportation					
Auto Loan/Lease 1					
Auto Loan/Lease 2					
Gas					
Maintenance					
Registration					
Inspection/Emissions					
Total Transportation Expenses					
Insurance					
Auto					
Home					
Life					
Disability					
Health					
CHIP					
Other Insurance_____					
Total Insurance Expenses					
Health and Medical					
Prescriptions					
Out of Pocket Medical Expenses					
Dental Expenses					
Vision Expenses					
Vitamins					
Health Savings Account					
Total Health and Medical Expenses					
Debt					
Credit Card 1					
Credit Card 2					
Credit Card 3					
Home Equity Loan					
Home Equity Line of Credit					
Student Loan 1					
Student Loan 2					
Other Debt_____					
Other Debt_____					
Total Debt Expenses					
Personal					
Clothing					
Haircuts					
Products and Services					
Other Personal Expense_____					
Other Personal Expense_____					
Total Personal Expenses					

	Actual Amount	Due Date	Need or Want	Overdue?	Balance Owed
Entertainment/Recreation					
Cable/Satellite TV					
Movies					
Hobbies					
Vacation					
Subscriptions					
Apps					
Music Purchases					
Gifts					
Christmas Gifts					
Memberships					
Other Recreation Expense_____					
Other Recreation Expense_____					
Total Ent/Rec Expenses					
Pets					
Food					
Vet Expense					
Grooming					
Prescriptions					
Total Pet Expenses					
Miscellaneous					
Tuition					
Child Care					
Lottery					
Cigarettes					
Alcohol					
Other Miscellaneous Expense_____					
Other Miscellaneous Expense_____					
Total Miscellaneous Expenses					

Summary					
Total Income		**Step 9:** *Add all income together.*			
Total Expenses		**Step 10:** *Add together the total expense amount from each expense category.*			
Difference		**Step 11:** *Subtract the "Total Expense" box from the "Total Income" box to find your surplus or shortfall for the month.*			

Step 2:
Diagnosis

Chapter Preview

Goal
To clearly identify the financial problems you are facing.

Connection Points

1. Diagnosing your financial problems requires an honest self-evaluation of how well you have taken care of God's money.
2. This process will reveal the good and bad financial habits, priorities, and decisions you have made.
3. Rely on your Financial Coach to help you determine the best possible solution to each of your financial problem.

At this stage in the game, you should have completed the Income and Expense Worksheet. If you didn't, then do not pass go because there is no $200 waiting for you. You must go back and complete the worksheet. Really, it's that important. Why you ask? Good question.

If you have ever gone to the hospital, chances are you made it out alive. How? Because the doctors were able to figure out what was wrong with your body, treat it, and then send you home. The doctors knew how to make you better because they asked you questions and put you through a series of tests, all to figure out what was going on inside your body. Then and only then were they able to treat the problem, thus making you better.

The same is true with your finances. In order to diagnose what financial problem(s) you have, questions need to be asked and tests need to be run. Perhaps, the best test you can run is the Income and Expense Worksheet. It is the x-ray of your finances. It shows what's coming in and what's going out. It also reveals your financial habits, priorities, and decisions. The information it provides, however, is only as good as the time and effort you put into it. So, please make sure that you thought of everything and did not leave out any income source, expense, or debt regardless of how old or insignificant you may think it is.

ACTION STEP 1:
Refer to the Genesis Financial Income and Expense Worksheet to answer the following questions:

1. What challenges did you face in completing the Income and Expense Worksheet?

_____

_____

2. How difficult was it to find and correctly list all of your bills and expenses?

_____

3. How much money was leftover after you subtracted your expenses from your income? $ _____

4. What reaction did you have when you saw how much money was leftover after you subtracted your expenses from your income? _____

_____

5. What does the worksheet reveal about your income? _____

_____

6. What does the worksheet reveal about your expenses? _____

_____

7. Are there habits or choices you are rethinking now that you have seen your whole financial situation on paper? _____

_____

8. Based on bills and expenses, what are your greatest priorities? _____

_____

9. How is your financial situation affecting you and those you love? _____

_____

10. How would you rate your overall financial situation? _____

11. How desperate and willing are you to make the changes and sacrifices necessary to turn your financial situation around? _____

So, what's your diagnosis: Too little income? Too many expenses? Are your priorities out of order? Chances are, you could be suffering from any number of financial problems. You should learn something from the worksheet and how you answered those eleven questions. In *Genesis Financial Workbook*, our concern is providing you with enough of the basics to get started. The Kingdom Crossroads class and/or a Financial Coach will dig deeper to provide you with the knowledge you need to take your finances to the next level. For now, many of the financial problems you are experiencing will be treated in Steps 3-8. If you are ready to begin treatment, let's move on to Step 3.

Step 3:
Go Positive

Chapter Preview

Goal
Commit to having a surplus at month's end by making realistic changes to your income and expenses.

Connection Points

1. Your monthly expenses must be less than your monthly income.
2. While there are a number of ways to adjust your income and expenses to achieve a surplus at month's end, it requires the 4 Ds on your part to make it consistent.
3. Be content with what God has given you but be discontent with the unwise financial decisions and habits that have led to your current financial situation.
4. One of the hardest things to do is telling yourself "No!" It also happens to be one of the most successful strategies to get your finances in order.

ACTION STEP 1:
Choose which of the following individuals is in a better financial situation.

1. Brad: Income = $1,700 per month and Expenses = $1,800 per month
2. Sara: Income = $1,300 per month and Expenses = $1,200 per month

What three things could Brad do to improve his financial situation?

1. _____
2. _____
3. _____

Step 3 is titled **"Go Positive"** because treating your financial problems begins with you stopping being negative and starting being positive. No, I'm not talking about your attitude but how much money you have leftover at the end of the month. You need to bring that number into positive territory, and if you think you can skip this section because you already have a positive balance at the end of the month, then think again. Surely, there are things in this section that could help you increase that number, and the first thing you must know is a complicated mathematical formula:

- **Income – Expenses = A Positive Number**

Okay, so the math isn't complicated but what can be a challenge is applying this to your own financial situation. It's easy to look at the action step above and see that Brad isn't positive at the end of the month, and then make recommendations for him to either increase income, cut expenses, or do both — but when you are in this situation, it is much more difficult. What expenses get cut? Where do I find another job? What needs to change so you go positive? The answers aren't easy. Frankly, you won't make any changes to income or expenses until you are desperate — until you realize that what you are doing right now is not working and continuing to do it will leave you digging a bigger and bigger hole for yourself.

The goal is to *go positive*. Nothing short of it will do and it will be impossible to reach this goal if you don't admit that what you are doing right now is not working. You can't keep doing the same things expecting different results. A new plan needs to formed. It will involve big changes and sacrifices, but what great and worthy goal has ever been easy to achieve? It's time to begin doing what others are unwilling to do. It's time to begin treating your financial problems. So, if you are ready, let's begin our journey to **go positive**! Take a look at Action Step 2.

ACTION STEP 2:

Refer to the Genesis Financial Income and Expense Worksheet and answer the following questions:

1. Do you have income? If so, from where? _____
    If you don't have any income, what are you doing to solve that problem? _____
    _____

2. What factors could affect your income in the next month to one year (temporary employment, certain benefits ending or beginning, new job, etc.)? _____
    _____

3. In addition to your current income, what other ways can you increase your income?
    _____

4. When you subtracted your total expenses from your total income, was there a surplus or deficit?
    _____

5. What did that surplus or deficit reveal to you about your financial situation?
    _____
    _____

6. How much additional income would you need to bring your final number into the positive?
    _____

7. How much would you need to cut from expenses to bring your final number into the positive?
    _____

8. How many bills and expenses were labeled as "Needs" versus "Wants?" _____ Needs _____ Wants

9. If you removed the bills and expenses labeled as "Wants," how would that affect the surplus or deficit?

   _____

10. If there is still a deficit after removing the "Wants" from your worksheet, what else can you do to bring your income and expenses into balance? Get creative!

    _____

    _____

11. Are there less expensive alternatives to your bills and expenses labeled "Needs?" If so, what are they?

    Need - _____ Cost - _____ Alternative - _____ Cost - _____
    Need - _____ Cost - _____ Alternative - _____ Cost - _____
    Need - _____ Cost - _____ Alternative - _____ Cost - _____
    Need - _____ Cost - _____ Alternative - _____ Cost - _____
    Need - _____ Cost - _____ Alternative - _____ Cost - _____
    Need - _____ Cost - _____ Alternative - _____ Cost - _____
    Need - _____ Cost - _____ Alternative - _____ Cost - _____
    Need - _____ Cost - _____ Alternative - _____ Cost - _____

    Total Cost for Needs: _____ **Total Cost for Alternatives:** _____

12. While choosing less expensive alternatives might affect your lifestyle, would they bring you into a surplus on your worksheet?

    _____

13. How many bills, expenses, and debts are labeled as "Overdue?"

    _____

14. What plan do you have to bring your past due bills and expenses current?

    _____

    _____

15. What part of the month do most of your bills and expenses fall?

    _____

    Income?

    _____

These questions were not asked for informational purposes. They were asked to get you thinking about the three ways to go positive: Increase the amount of income, decrease the amount of expenses, or do both. You need to get creative and even desperate to make this happen. Here are some suggestions:

Increase your income

- Ask for a raise or get trained for the next position up from your current position.
- Sit down with your employer and explain your financial situation. Who knows what opportunities they might make available to you — whether it's just extra hours or the company pays for college classes, which could get you a better job down the line.
- Apply for other jobs that pay more.
- Get a second job at night or on the weekends.
- Ask your self-employed friends if they have any odd jobs you could do in your spare time.
- Turn your hobby into a part-time job.

Decrease your expenses

- Cut the amount you spend on groceries.
- Shop at discount grocery stores.
- Clip coupons
- Create a menu of all the meals you will have over the next two weeks and shop with a grocery list with just those ingredients.
- Stop eating out; *yes, even fast food.*
- Have a car? Sell it and walk or take public transportation.
- Find a cheaper apartment.
- Ask the landlord of your apartment to decrease the rent in exchange for you doing the yard work, snow removal, and other small jobs.
- Switch your smartphone for a "dumbphone" on a prepaid plan.
- Ask to be added to a friend's cell phone plan and do a chore for them in exchange for them paying for your minutes.
- Find cheaper alternatives to everything.

Many of the things listed will only be contenders if you are fed up with your current financial situation. I mean *really* fed up. The funny thing is that when you are really desperate, you are willing to do things that wouldn't have even crossed your mind weeks ago. It's good to be unhappy with where you are and it is good to be desperate. Be content with what you have and live within your means, but be discontent with your unwise financial decisions and a lifestyle that doesn't reflect good stewardship. A fire needs to grow in you; a passion to take control of your money and no longer allow it to tell you what to do. *A warning*: *You can't start something like this for a month and get tired of it and quit.* You have to make a promise to yourself that you won't quit when it gets hard; that you won't give up when you are tired from your second job; that you won't give in when your belly is growling because the junk food drawer in your kitchen is empty, leading you to buy out the chip aisle at the grocery store. You don't need the fast food. You don't need the fancy phone. You don't need cable. You don't need the Internet (almost every public library has it for free). You need to tell yourself "NO!" Then and only then will you stop being negative and start going positive.

> Be content with what you have and live within your means, but be discontent with your unwise financial decisions and a lifestyle that doesn't reflect good stewardship.

To help you with this, see Action Step 3 where you will begin revising the Genesis Financial Income and Expense Worksheet using the revised version. While this revised version looks the same, its purpose is different. Now, your goal is to find a way to go positive. Revise your income, expenses, or both. Take the suggestions above and give them a try. Whatever you do, make sure your revisions are realistic, can be done quickly, and bring you to a positive number.

ACTION STEP 3:

1. Use the Genesis Financial Revised Income and Expense Worksheet to go positive.

When you are positive on your Revised Income and Expense Worksheet, then it is time to transfer the final product to the Genesis Financial Finalized Income and Expense Worksheet. Keep this finalized version handy because it will be used later. Now, you can move on to **Step 4**.

Concept Review

1. Going Positive

Keys for Understanding
➢ Going positive is not simply a math exercise of making cuts to expenses in order to show a surplus.
➢ In order to go positive and *stay* positive, you must understand and practice stewardship, live within your means, be content, prioritize your needs above your wants, and pray.
➢ The changes you made to your income and expenses to arrive at a positive number need to be **realistic** and **workable**. This means that you can actually do what you are saying on paper. For example, if your showing a $200 deficit you can cut your grocery budget from $600 a month to $300 a month. This will bring you to a positive number, but is $300 going to buy enough food so you don't starve? Is it realistic?
➢ The most realistic and workable way to go positive monthly is cutting out expenses labeled as "wants" and making small reductions to many expenses labeled as "needs."
➢ In certain circumstances, major changes may need to take place like selling an extra car, quitting smoking, or moving to a cheaper home or apartment. Nothing is off the table to go positive.

Genesis Financial Tip:

Your Financial Coach — A personal trainer for your finances

Your Financial Coach is a wealth of information. They are here to teach the truth about money — God's truth. They will challenge you to make the difficult but rewarding financial decisions. They will encourage you when you find it hard to say no to yourself. And, they will be praying for you because none of this can be done without God. So, make every effort to listen to your Financial Coach and learn from what they teach. You can thank them later for it!

Genesis Financial *Revised* Income and Expense Worksheet

The Genesis Financial *Revised* Income and Expense Worksheet gives you the chance to revise the income and expenses from your initial worksheet so that you end up with a surplus at the end. Achieving a surplus is Step 3 in the "Steps to Financial Stability." Remember, your goal is to go positive. So, make realistic adjustments to your income and expenses until there is a surplus at the end, or grow it if it already exists.

Income

	Actual Amount	Pay Date 1	Pay Date 2	Pay Date 3
Wage/Salary 1 _____				
Wage/Salary 2 _____				
Social Security _____				
Unemployment _____				
Child Support _____				
Miscellaneous Income _____				
Total Income				

Expenses

	Actual Amount	Due Date	Need or Want	Overdue?	Balance Owed
Giving, Offerings and Charities					
Giving 1:_____					
Giving 2:_____					
Giving 3:_____					
Giving 4:_____					
Total Giving					
Paying Yourself					
Investments					
Savings Account					
Emergency Savings Account					
Total Savings					
Living Expenses					
Mortgage/Rent					
Real Estate Tax					
School Tax					
Maintenance					
Other Living Expense _____					
Other Living Expense _____					
Total Living Expenses					
Food					
SNAP (food stamps do not count as expense)					
Groceries					
Dining Out					
Total Food Expenses					

	Actual Amount	Due Date	Need or Want	Overdue?	Balance Owed
Utilities					
Water					
Sewer					
Electric					
Natural Gas					
Cell Phone					
Internet					
Other Utility_____					
Total Utility Expenses					
Transportation					
Auto Loan/Lease 1					
Auto Loan/Lease 2					
Gas					
Maintenance					
Registration					
Inspection/Emissions					
Total Transportation Expenses					
Insurance					
Auto					
Home					
Life					
Disability					
Health					
CHIP					
Other Insurance_____					
Total Insurance Expenses					
Health and Medical					
Prescriptions					
Out of Pocket Medical Expenses					
Dental Expenses					
Vision Expenses					
Vitamins					
Health Savings Account					
Total Health and Medical Expenses					
Debt					
Credit Card 1					
Credit Card 2					
Credit Card 3					
Home Equity Loan					
Home Equity Line of Credit					
Student Loan 1					
Student Loan 2					
Other Debt_____					
Other Debt_____					
Total Debt Expenses					

	Actual Amount	Due Date	Need or Want	Overdue?	Balance Owed
Personal					
Clothing					
Haircuts					
Products and Services					
Other Personal Expense_____					
Other Personal Expense_____					
Total Personal Expenses					
Entertainment/Recreation					
Cable/Satellite TV					
Movies					
Hobbies					
Vacation					
Subscriptions					
Apps					
Music Purchases					
Gifts					
Christmas Gifts					
Memberships					
Other Recreation Expense_____					
Other Recreation Expense_____					
Total Ent/Rec Expenses					
Pets					
Food					
Vet Expense					
Grooming					
Prescriptions					
Total Pet Expenses					
Miscellaneous					
Tuition					
Child Care					
Lottery					
Cigarettes					
Alcohol					
Other Miscellaneous Expense_____					
Other Miscellaneous Expense_____					
Total Miscellaneous Expenses					

Summary					
Total Income					
Total Expenses					
Difference					

Genesis Financial *Finalized* Income and Expense Worksheet

This is the finalized version of the Genesis Financial Income and Expense Worksheet. Remember, this should have a surplus after all expenses have been paid.

Income

	Actual Amount	Pay Date 1	Pay Date 2	Pay Date 3
Wage/Salary 1 _____				
Wage/Salary 2 _____				
Social Security_____				
Unemployment_____				
Child Support_____				
Miscellaneous Income _____				
Total Income				

Expenses

	Actual Amount	Due Date	Need or Want	Overdue?	Balance Owed
Giving, Offerings, and Charities					
Giving 1:_____					
Giving 2:_____					
Giving 3:_____					
Giving 4:_____					
Total Giving					
Paying Yourself					
Investments					
Savings Account					
Emergency Savings Account					
Total Savings					
Living Expenses					
Mortgage/Rent					
Real Estate Tax					
School Tax					
Maintenance					
Other Living Expense _____					
Other Living Expense _____					
Total Living Expenses					
Food					
SNAP (food stamps do not count as expense)					
Groceries					
Dining Out					
Total Food Expenses					
Utilities					
Water					
Sewer					
Electric					
Natural Gas					
Cell Phone					
Internet					
Other Utility_____					
Total Utility Expenses					

	Actual Amount	Due Date	Need or Want	Overdue?	Balance Owed
Transportation					
Auto Loan/Lease 1					
Auto Loan/Lease 2					
Gas					
Maintenance					
Registration					
Inspection/Emissions					
Total Transportation Expenses					
Insurance					
Auto					
Home					
Life					
Disability					
Health					
CHIP					
Other Insurance_____					
Total Insurance Expenses					
Health and Medical					
Prescriptions					
Out of Pocket Medical Expenses					
Dental Expenses					
Vision Expenses					
Vitamins					
Health Savings Account					
Total Health and Medical Expenses					
Debt					
Credit Card 1					
Credit Card 2					
Credit Card 3					
Home Equity Loan					
Home Equity Line of Credit					
Student Loan 1					
Student Loan 2					
Other Debt_____					
Other Debt_____					
Total Debt Expenses					
Personal					
Clothing					
Haircuts					
Products and Services					
Other Personal Expense_____					
Other Personal Expense_____					
Total Personal Expenses					

	Actual Amount	Due Date	Need or Want	Overdue?	Balance Owed
Entertainment/Recreation					
Cable/Satellite TV					
Movies					
Hobbies					
Vacation					
Subscriptions					
Apps					
Music Purchases					
Gifts					
Christmas Gifts					
Memberships					
Other Recreation Expense_____					
Other Recreation Expense_____					
Total Ent/Rec Expenses					
Pets					
Food					
Vet Expense					
Grooming					
Prescriptions					
Total Pet Expenses					
Miscellaneous					
Tuition					
Child Care					
Lottery					
Cigarettes					
Alcohol					
Other Miscellaneous Expense_____					
Other Miscellaneous Expense_____					
Total Miscellaneous Expenses					

Summary					
Total Income					
Total Expenses					
Difference					

Step 4:
Build an Emergency Fund

Chapter Preview

Goal

Plan for the unexpected by beginning to save money in an emergency fund.

Connection Points

1. Life is filled with unexpected expenses that can derail your financial plan.
2. An emergency fund is the way you plan for the "unplanned."
3. You begin by saving your monthly surplus until you reach the initial savings goal you and your Financial Coach have set.
4. Your emergency fund is for emergencies only and not to be used unwisely.

ACTION STEP 1:

1. How do you currently pay for unexpected bills like auto repairs or medical bills?

   _____

2. If you missed a few days at work because of an illness, how would you make up the difference to pay for all of your bills and expenses?

   _____

   If you live on earth, you know that nothing goes exactly as you plan it. In fact, the only thing you can expect is to expect the unexpected. But when it comes to your money, the unexpected is often not very good. The unexpected flat tire or the unexpected trip to the doctor can throw your finances into chaos and make you question how you will pay for everything.

   Going positive was a giant step forward on your way towards recovery from your financial problems, but it can go south pretty quickly when the unexpected hits. So, to prevent you from heading backwards into negative territory, you need to start an "**emergency fund**."

   An emergency fund is exactly what it sounds like — a place where extra money is kept for emergencies. How do you start an emergency fund and where do you put it? Good question. In the last step called "Go Positive," you did some amazing things and made huge changes, so you would have money leftover at the end of the month. Now, it's time to tell that extra money where to go — into your new emergency fund.

How you start your emergency fund – Your entire surplus should go directly into an emergency fund until you have saved $250. That's not the only way to save for your new emergency fund, though. Find ways to kickstart it like selling stuff you don't use anymore, a tax refund, or some other creative way. For example, let's say you sell some stuff and earn $75 and have a surplus of $50 every month. It will take you roughly three months to save your emergency fund goal of $250. Set a goal to have the emergency fund fully funded in one to three months. Anything longer than that and it will fall off your list of priorities.

Where you put the emergency fund – Where you put it can vary based on where you live, but the best place to do it is in a free savings account at a local bank, with no deposit and no minimum balance requirements. This could be hard to find, so your next step is to stick it into a free checking account and decline any offer for a debit card or checks that would give you easy access to your emergency fund. Warning: Do not keep this money in your pocket, wallet, purse, or any other place it can be easily accessed. If you are not super disciplined, you will spend it on a hamburger and French fries and those are not emergencies.

> *An emergency fund is exactly what it sounds like — a place where extra money is kept for emergencies.*
>
> *Set a goal to have the emergency fund fully funded in one to three months.*

So, what is an *emergency*? It's important to know this and set rules so that you know when you should and when you should not use the money.

- **What it is**: An emergency is anything that will derail your budget (covered in a later step). If the income you planned on is unexpectedly less, or your bills and expenses are unexpectedly more, then you may use your emergency fund. However, the next month, you must begin to replenish your emergency fund, bringing it back to $250.
- **What it isn't**: An emergency is not something you want that was not listed on your budget (again, covered in a later step). The emergency fund is not there for you to fall back on to make unwise impulse purchases.

The bottom line is that you worked too hard to get yourself positive to use your emergency fund unwisely. So, if you run into a situation where you want to use your emergency fund, follow these rules:

> **Rule 1**: Contact your Financial Coach immediately. Let them know what is going on and seek their advice for the best plan.
>
> **Rule 2**: If you don't have a Financial Coach, wait at least one day before withdrawing money from the emergency fund account. This will allow you to see things more clearly and make a wiser decision.
>
> **Rule 3**: Pray. Ask the Lord for wisdom and help to make the right decision. You can never go wrong when you include God into any financial situation.

It is crucial for you to accomplish the goal of saving $250 as fast as you can. How quickly you reach it will determine how quickly you can move on to address other areas of your finances discussed in later sections of the workbook. In the Kingdom Crossroads Class, we will discuss higher savings goals for your emergency fund. For now, focus your effort on saving $250 and then stay disciplined to use it properly and replenish it when used.

Concept Review

1. Planning for the Unexpected

> **_Keys for Understanding_**
> ➤ Because you can't plan for everything, a good financial plan will include saving for the unexpected in something called an emergency fund.
> ➤ An adequately funded emergency fund will provide the money for unexpected medical bills, car repairs, or even a job loss.
> ➤ Emergency funds will help you to stay positive and not use credit cards.

2. Building an Emergency Fund

> **_Keys for Understanding_**
> ➤ _How to save for your emergency fund?_ Begin saving for your emergency fund by saving your leftover surplus at the end of the month until you have reached a goal of $250 (the goal can vary based on each person). Try and think of other ways to reach this goal more quickly like selling items you own but don't use anymore.
> ➤ _Where to save your emergency fund?_ Go to your local bank and ask what accounts they have which are free to open and carry no minimum balance. Also, decline a debit card or checks that could be tied to the account.

3. Using an Emergency Fund

> **_Keys for Understanding_**
> ➤ You should use your emergency fund for emergencies.
> ➤ _What is an emergency?_ An emergency is an unexpected shift in income or an unplanned expense not originally budgeted that causes you to be short at the end of the month.
> ➤ _What is not an emergency?_ Non-emergencies are when you desire to buy something you want but didn't plan for in your budget.
> ➤ Make sure you contact your Financial Coach before using your emergency fund.
> ➤ Exhaust every other option before using your emergency fund, but do not use credit cards.
> ➤ Pray and ask for wisdom and guidance from the Lord for the best way to handle unexpected financial situations.

Step 5:
The Genesis Monthly Budget
and Budget Schedule

Goal

Create your Genesis Monthly Budget and Budget Schedule.

Connection Points

1. The Genesis Monthly Budget is the first step in your regular and ongoing plan towards better financial stewardship.
2. A budget allows you plan your expected income and expenses for a month and then compare them to what you received and paid out.
3. The Genesis Monthly Budget Schedule organizes the expenses listed on your monthly budget into tables based on when your income will be paid to you.
4. A budget schedule is the plan you follow to pay your monthly bills
5. Your Genesis Monthly Budget and Budget Schedule will help you tell your money where to go BEFORE you get paid, not AFTER you get paid.

Genesis Monthly Budget

In "Me, Myself, and God's Money," you learned that you are a steward of God's money. God is giving you something that is His and asking you to be responsible for it. That's a big deal! Because of how big a deal this is, don't you think it would be wise to have a plan for that money to follow? A plan that lists everything your income must pay for the month?

This plan is called a Budget. A budget is a great tool to help you manage your money every month. It is a list of all the income and expenses you *plan* to have in a month and compares it to what you *actually* receive in income and pay in expenses. Your budget is a snapshot of everything you plan on doing with your money every month. You set the course and the budget allows you to keep track of how closely you are following that course.

This may sound like it's difficult to create and keep track of, but it's not. The simplicity of the Genesis Monthly Budget is that you have done almost all of the work when you completed the Genesis Financial Finalized Income and Expense Worksheet. All of your income, expenses, amounts, and due dates from your Finalized Income and Expense Worksheet will become a part of the Genesis Monthly Budget. In fact, the first six steps in completing the Genesis Monthly Budget will entail you transferring information from your Finalized Income and Expense

Worksheet onto the Monthly Budget. For all future budgets, they should be completed before the end of the month based on the income and expenses you expect to have for the following month. For example, September's budget would be completed during the last week of August based on the income and expense you expect to have in September. It's important to complete next month's budget during the last week of the current month. This will take the guesswork and uncertainty out of what next month's finances will look like.

ACTION STEP 1:

1. Refer to the Finalized Income and Expense Worksheet and follow the instructions to complete Steps 1-7 of the Genesis Monthly Budget. Please make sure you only use monthly amounts for income and expenses. For some help, please see the examples at the end of this chapter.

GENESIS MONTHLY BUDGET

Please refer to the Genesis Financial Finalized Income and Expense Worksheet for all income, expenses, and their related due dates. Follow each step in order with Genesis Budget Schedule in handy in the Steps 8 and 9.

Summary	Amount	
Expected Balance (Total Expected Income - Total Expected Expenses)		**Step 7** Subtract the total Expected Expenses from the total Expected Income. **Stop here and read the book's section titled "Genesis Monthly Budget Schedule."**
Actual Balance (Total Actual Income - Total Actual Expenses)		**Step 13** Subtract the total Actual Expenses from the total Actual Income

Income

	Step 1	Step 2	Step 3				Step 8	Step 10
	List all income sources for the month.	Fill in the amount of income you EXPECT to receive from each income source. **Make sure the amounts are monthly.** Then, add them together and place that total amount in the Total Income box.	List the next four dates you will be paid.				Refer to the "Genesis Financial Budget Schedule." Place the table number each income source will fall into based on its pay date .	When you are paid, fill in the amount you ACTUALLY received from each income source. Add them together and place the total in the Total Income box. Then, complete **Step** 5 on the "Genesis Financial Budget Schedule."
	Income Source	Expected Amount	Pay Date 1	Pay Date 2	Pay Date 3	Pay Date 4	Table	Actual Amount
1								
2								
3								
4								
5								
6								
	Total Income							

Expenses

	Step 4	Step 5	Step 6	Step 9	Step 11	Step 12
	List all expenses for the month.	Fill in the amount you EXPECT to pay for the expense. **Make sure the amounts are monthly.** Then, add them together and place that total amount in the Total Expense box.	List each expense's due date.	Refer to the "Genesis Financial Budget Schedule." Place the table number each expense source will fall in based on its expected amount and due date.	When you receive the ACTUAL amount due for each expense, list it here. Then, complete Step 5 on the "Genesis Financial Budget Schedule."	List the date you paid the expense.
	Expense	Expected Amount	Due Date	Table	Actual Amount	Paid Date
1						
2						
3						
4						
5						
6						
7						
8						
9						
10						
11						
12						
13						
14						
15						
16						
17						
18						
19						
20						
21						
22						
23						
24						
25						
26						
27						
28						
29						
30						
31						
32						
Total Expenses						

As you can see the budget is you telling your money where to go BEFORE you get paid, not AFTER you get paid. It is a set of instructions that your money must follow every month based on your needs and priorities.

> *A budget tells you what bills need to be paid every month...a budget schedule tells you how to pay your bills every month.*

It is also a great tool to help you become a great steward of God's money. But, while it is a great tool, it has its shortcomings.

The problem with most budget plans is that they show your income and your expenses as if they are all received at one time. And you know this is not true because you get paid at different times throughout the month and your expenses are due at different times throughout the month. So, a budget can organize everything into one place, but to make a budget work in the real world, it must flow into a schedule that organizes your expenses according to when you get paid and how much you are paid.

This is where the **Genesis Monthly Budget Schedule** comes in. This handy tool will organize your expenses into tables based on when you are paid. This way, each expense can be assigned to a specific paycheck in the month — *but always before the expense's due date*. The Budget Schedule brings your budget into the real world and makes it usable.

A budget tells you *what* bills need to be paid every month while a budget schedule tells you *how* to pay your bills every month. But how do you set it up? It's simple. Below you will see an example of a budget schedule:

Table 1						Table 2				
Pay Date _____						**Pay Date** _____				
	Amount						Amount			
Available Balance						**Available Balance**				
Income						**Income**				
Total						Total				
Expenses	Amount Due	Due Date	Amount Paid	Date Paid		Expenses	Amount Due	Due Date	Amount Paid	Date Paid
Total Expenses						Total Expenses				
Total Income						Total Income				
Total Expenses						Total Expenses				
Surplus						Surplus				

At first, they may just look like two tables. Income at the top, expenses in the middle, and a summary at the bottom. But in a moment, you will see how the information from your monthly budget transfers into these two tables to create a workable monthly plan that puts you in the driver's seat of your finances. Because of how important the Budget Schedule is, we will look at each portion of the tables so that you have a clear understanding of how it works.

Tables and Income

One of the first things you will need to decide is how many tables you will need for your budget worksheet. This amount will be determined by the frequency of your pay. Each paycheck will typically have its own table. So, if you are paid biweekly you will have two tables per month since you are paid twice a month. For the two months out of the year biweekly pay recipients receive three checks, they will have three tables. There are exceptions to this like if you are married or you receive multiple paychecks around the same date. Here are some general rules on how many tables you will need:

- **Biweekly** – If you are paid biweekly then you will typically have two tables per month with a third table for during the two months out of the year you receive three paychecks.
- **Weekly** – If you are paid weekly you will have four tables.
- **Semimonthly** – Those paid semimonthly will always have two tables.
- **Married/Two or more paychecks in one week** – If you are married or simply have multiple paychecks being paid around the same date, you may list those paychecks under one table.
- **Monthly** – If you are paid monthly then you will only need one table, or you may simply use the budget and forgo the table. This is typical for those who receive Social Security.

For our example, Peter and Mary are married and are paid on different days but in the same week. So we will only need two tables. Then, we fill in the dates they will be paid in the upper section of the table labeled "Pay Date." Below that, we fill in the income source and amount.

Table 1						Table 2				
Pay Date: 8/4 & 8/5						Pay Date: 8/18 & 8/19				
	Amount						Amount			
Available Balance	$0.00					Available Balance	$0.00			
Income						Income				
Peter's Pay	$1,325.00					Peter's Pay	$1,325.00			
Mary's Pay	$850.00					Mary's Pay	$850.00			
Total	$2,175.00					Total	$2,175.00			

The **Available Balance** row should only be filled in if there is leftover money in your checking account at the end of the month. If you fill in a dollar amount in this row, make sure that all checks have cleared and there are no pending debit card transactions yet to be subtracted. Once your income section is complete, add it to any available balance and list it as your **Total Income**.

Expenses and Summary

Now that the income portion of our budget schedule is complete, we can move onto the expense portion. This is where we begin to see the advantage of the budget schedule over the monthly budget. To begin, take a look at the expenses on your monthly budget and pay close attention to the due date of each expense. You will be assigning each expense in your monthly budget to one of your tables based on when the bill's due date falls compared to the table's pay dates. In our example of Peter and Mary, all the expenses from their monthly budget have been placed in the table that best fits the due date and amount due. Take a look:

Table 1				
Pay Date: August 4th & 5th				
	Expected Amount		Actual Amount	
Available Balance	$0.00			
Income				
Peter's Job	$1,325.00			
Mary's Job	$850.00			
Total	**$2,175.00**			

Expenses	Amount Due	Due Date	Amount Paid	Date Paid
Dining out	$50.00	8/5/2017		
Trash	$25.00	8/5/2017		
Auto Fuel	$75.00	8/5/2017		
Emergency Savings	$50.00	8/5/2017		
Savings	$50.00	8/5/2017		
Groceries	$400.00	8/6/2017		
Giving	$275.00	8/7/2017		
Credit Card 2	$80.00	8/7/2017		
Car Loan 1	$200.00	8/8/2017		
Cable/Internet	$180.00	8/10/2017		
Cell Phone	$175.00	8/11/2017		
Sewer	$45.00	8/12/2017		
Missionary Sponsorship	$50.00	8/15/2017		
Auto Insurance	$80.00	8/15/2017		
Life Insurance	$40.00	8/15/2017		
Haircuts	$60.00	8/15/2017		
Total Expenses	$1,835.00			

Total Income	**$2,175.00**			
Total Expenses	$1,835.00			
Surplus*	**$340.00**			

*All or part of the Surplus from Table 1 becomes the available balance in Table 2.

Table 2				
Pay Date: August 18th & 19th				
	Expected Amount		Actual Amount	
Available Balance	$320.00			
Income				
Peter's Job	$1,325.00			
Mary's Job	$850.00			
Total	**$2,495.00**			

Expenses	Amount Due	Due Date	Amount Paid	Date Paid
Electric	$100.00	8/18/2017		
Dining out	$50.00	8/19/2017		
Water	$35.00	8/19/2017		
Auto Fuel	$75.00	8/19/2017		
Emergency Savings	$50.00	8/19/2017		
Savings	$50.00	8/19/2017		
Groceries	$400.00	8/20/2017		
Pet Food	$40.00	8/20/2017		
Child Care	$250.00	8/20/2017		
Giving	$275.00	8/21/2017		
Heat - gas	$65.00	8/21/2017		
Medications	$35.00	8/28/2017		
Mortgage*	$775.00	9/1/2017		
Car Maintenance	$25.00	9/1/2017		
Out of Pocket Medical	$40.00	9/1/2017		
Gifts (B-day/Christmas)	$60.00	9/1/2017		
Vacation	$100.00	9/1/2017		
Credit Card 1	$65.00	9/1/2017		
	$2,490.00			

Total Income	**$2,495.00**			
Total Expenses	$2,490.00			
Surplus**	**$5.00**			

*The mortgage payment could have been split between the two tables as an alternate way of covering this large expense.

**All or part of the Surplus from Table 2 becomes the available balance for next month's Table 1.

Notice how all the bills for the month are listed in one of the two tables. There are some bills coming due in September which are best paid in August since they are due before the first pay in September. Here are some helpful rules and tips to help you decide in which table an expense should go.

Rules for assigning expenses to a table
- **Rule 1** – Each expense should be placed in a table where the expense's due date comes after the pay date. Otherwise, the bill would be paid late.
- **Rule 2** – You must place an expense in a table where there is enough income to cover the amount due. This may require some shuffling of expenses from one table to another but remember that all bills must be paid on time.
- **Rule 3** – A table's total income plus any available balance must be equal to or greater than the sum of the same table's expenses. This is pretty straightforward but to restate it: You can't have more total expenses than total income. If you do, you will break the table.
- **Rule 4** – Any surplus in Table 1 becomes the available balance in Table 2. An available balance in Table 2 would be passed on to available balance in Table 1 of the following month, *or* Table 3 if a third table is necessary for the current month.

Tips for assigning expenses to a table

- **Tip 1** – Bills and expenses that are due in the first five days of the month may be better off when paired with the last pay from the previous month.
- **Tip 2** – If your pay varies through the month, consider matching bigger expenses with bigger income even if that bigger bill isn't due for a while.
- **Tip 3** – Consider splitting bigger bills among two or even three tables and keep the money in your checking account until the bill is due.

Part of assigning each expense into a paycheck's table is determining if there is enough income to cover the expense. After you assign multiple expenses into a table, you should begin to add up the table's expenses to make sure the sum of the expenses does not exceed the total income of that table. This may require some shuffling of expenses and possibly paying a bill much earlier than due in order to make it fit. That's okay! Remember, keep adding your expenses until all expenses are accounted for. And yes, every expense should fit without a problem because you have a surplus in your monthly budget.

The last thing you do is close out your tables by subtracting your total expenses from your total income. See the example from Pater and Mary:

Total Income	$2,175.00				Total Income	$2,495.00		
Total Expenses	$1,835.00				Total Expenses	$2,490.00		
Surplus*	$340.00				Surplus**	$5.00		

Any surplus from Table 1 become the available balance of Table 2. If there is a surplus in Table 2 then it becomes the available balance of next month's Table 1. However, if you needed a third table for the month, then the surplus from Table 2 become the available balance for Table 3.

Now it's time to give it a try on your own using the information from your monthly budget.

ACTION STEP 2:

1. Complete Steps 1-4 of the Genesis Monthly Budget Schedule. Please make sure you only use monthly amounts for income and expenses. If you need more than the three tables in the worksheet, see the Appendix for a four-table monthly budget schedule.

GENESIS MONTHLY BUDGET SCHEDULE

The Genesis Monthly Budget Schedule will help organize and plan your finances, so that you know *how* and *when* to pay your bills. Refer to the Genesis Financial Budget Worksheet for amounts and due dates.

→ Step 1: Pay Date, Income, and Amount - Refer to the Genesis Financial Budget Worksheet. Fill in the "Pay Date." This refers to the dates throughout the month you will be paid. Each table will have a different Pay Date. So, in Table 1, the first pay date would go in along with the description of the pay under the "Income" column and the amount of the pay in the "Amount" column. If you have multiple paychecks around the same date, place them in the same Table. Do the same for Table 2 and Table 3 with pay dates falling in the middle and end of the month.

→ Step 2: Expenses, Amount Due, and Due Date - Refer to the Genesis Financial Budget Worksheet. Begin placing expenses and the amounts into each table based on when the expense is due. Rule 1: Each expense should be placed in a table where the expense's due date comes after the pay date. Rule 2: You must only place the expenses in a table where there is enough income to cover the amount due. Helpful Hints: Bills and expenses that are due in the first five days of the month may be better off when paired with the last pay from the previous month. Also, if your pay varies through the month, consider matching bigger expenses with bigger income even if that bigger bill isn't due for a while. Also, consider splitting bigger bills among two or even three tables and keep the money in your checking account until the bill is due.

→ Step 3: Available Balance - This would include any money in your checking account or cash on hand. Warning: When filling in your available balance, please make sure that all checks and debit card purchases have cleared and there are no outstanding bills or expenses that need to be subtracted from that amount. Add this amount to your income in each table.

→ Step 4: Proofing Your Tables - When you have finished placing all income and expenses in the proper table, subtract the "Total Expenses" from the "Total Income" and place the amount in "Surplus." Make sure you are not negative in any table. If you are, then move an expense to a table with an earlier pay. When you have completed Steps 1-4 of the Budget Schedule, please go back to the monthly budget and complete Steps 8-9.

→ Step 5: Actual Amount and Amount Paid - When you receive your paycheck, place the actual amount received in the "Actual Amount" column. The amounts and totals should be the same as Step 10 in the "Genesis Financial Budget Worksheet." Under the expense portion of each table, complete the "Amount Paid" column with the actual amount of each expense from Step 11 of the "Genesis Financial Budget Worksheet."

Table 1

Pay Date _____

	Amount	Actual Amount
Available Balance		
Income		
Total		

Expenses	Amount Due	Due Date	Amount Paid	Date Paid
Total Expenses				

Total Income	
Total Expenses	
Surplus	

Table 2

Pay Date _____

	Amount	Actual Amount
Available Balance		
Income		
Total		

Expenses	Amount Due	Due Date	Amount Paid	Date Paid
Total Expenses				

Total Income	
Total Expenses	
Surplus	

Table 3

Pay Date _____

	Amount	Actual Amount
Available Balance		
Income		
Total		

Expenses	Amount Due	Due Date	Amount Paid	Date Paid
Total Expenses				

Total Income	
Total Expenses	
Surplus	

Now that you have completed the first four steps of the monthly budget schedule, it's time to go back to your monthly budget and complete Steps 8 and 9. Here, you will list the table number in the monthly budget that you assigned to each income and expense in the budget schedule.

ACTION STEP 3:

1. Go back to your Genesis Monthly Budget and complete Steps 8 and 9.

Finishing the Monthly Budget and Budget Schedule

So far, you have completed the first nine steps of the Genesis Monthly Budget and the first four steps of the Budget Schedule. These same steps will be completed before the beginning of each month. This is the planning phase. Before you ever enter the month, you will know exactly how you will pay every bill and when. It eliminates the uncertainty, chaos, and confusion that often comes when no plan is in place. It also allows you to properly handle the unexpected bill that comes up because your car breaks down or you had to take your child to the doctor. You will know exactly what you can afford up and above what you already planned for, and when to turn to your emergency account.

As you enter the new month and begin receiving income and paying bills, it's time to record the actual amounts you received and paid. Remember, up to this point, you were only using expected amounts for your income and expenses. Sometimes, your income and expenses vary from what you planned. So when you are actually paid, record those actual income amounts in the monthly budget first and then the budget schedule. When you begin to pay your bills, do the same thing. Record the actual amount of the bill in the monthly budget and then the budget schedule. Also, record the dates you paid each bill. Check out Peter and Mary's monthly budget and budget schedule to see how they handled recording their actual income and expenses:

Peter and Mary's Monthly Budget *with Actuals*

Summary	Amount
Expected Balance (Total Expected Income - Total Expected Expenses)	$25.00
Actual Balance (Total Actual Income - Total Actual Expenses)	$29.00

Income

	Income Source	Expected Amount	Pay Date 1	Pay Date 2	Pay Date 3	Pay Date 4	Table	Actual Amount
1	Peter's Job	$2,650 ($1325 per pay)	5-Aug	19-Aug			1 & 2	$2,650.00
2	Mary's Job	$1,700 ($850 per pay)	4-Aug	18-Aug			1 & 2	$1,700.00
3								
4								
5								
6								
	Total Income	$4,350.00						$4,350.00

Expenses

	Expense	Expected Amount	Due Date	Table	Actual Amount	Paid Date
1	Giving	$275.00	7th	1	$275.00	8/5
2	Giving	$275.00	21st	2	$275.00	8/19
3	Missionary Sponsorship	$50.00	15th	1	$50.00	8/5
4	Mortgage	$775.00	1st	2	$775.00	8/19
5	Groceries	$400.00	6th	1	$433.00	8/5
6	Groceries	$400.00	20th	2	$397.00	8/19
7	Dining out	$50.00	19th	2	$43.00	8/18
8	Dining out	$50.00	5th	1	$65.00	8/4
9	Water	$35.00	19th	2	$35.00	8/18
10	Sewer	$45.00	12th	1	$45.00	8/5
11	Electric	$100.00	18th	2	$114.00	8/18
12	Heat - gas	$65.00	21st	2	$58.00	8/19
13	Cell Phone	$175.00	11th	1	$179.00	8/5
14	Trash	$25.00	5th	1	$25.00	8/4
15	Car Loan 1	$200.00	8th	1	$200.00	8/5
16	Auto Fuel	$75.00	5th	1	$68.00	8/4
17	Auto Fuel	$75.00	19th	2	$89.00	8/18
18	Car Maintenance	$25.00	1st	2	$25.00	8/19
19	Auto Insurance	$80.00	15th	1	$80.00	8/5
20	Life Insurance	$40.00	15th	1	$40.00	8/5
21	Medications	$35.00	28th	2	$35.00	8/19
22	Out of Pocket Medical	$40.00	1st	2	$40.00	8/19
23	Credit Card 1	$65.00	1st	2	$65.00	8/19
24	Credit Card 2	$80.00	7th	1	$80.00	8/5
25	Haircuts	$60.00	15th	1	$60.00	8/5
26	Cable/Internet	$180.00	10th	1	$180.00	8/5
27	Gifts (B-day/Christmas)	$60.00	1st	2	$60.00	8/19
28	Vacation	$100.00	1st	2	$100.00	8/19
29	Pet Food	$40.00	20th	2	$40.00	8/19
30	Child Care	$250.00	20th	2	$250.00	8/19
31	Emergency Savings	$50.00	5th	1	$50.00	8/4
32	Emergency Savings	$50.00	19th	2	$40.00	8/18
33	Savings	$50.00	19th	2	$0.00	Did not pay
34	Savings	$50.00	5th	1	$50.00	8/4
	Total Expenses	$4,325.00			$4,321.00	

Peter and Mary's Budget Schedule *with Actuals*

Table 1

Pay Date: August 4th & 5th

	Expected Amount		Actual Amount	
Available Balance	$15.00		$15.00	
Income				
Peter's Job	$1,325.00		$1,325.00	
Mary's Job	$850.00		$850.00	
Total	**$2,190.00**		$2,190.00	

Expenses	Amount Due	Due Date	Amount Paid	Date Paid
Dining out	$50.00	8/5	$65.00	8/4
Trash	$25.00	8/5	$25.00	8/4
Auto Fuel	$75.00	8/5	$68.00	8/4
Emergency Savings	$50.00	8/5	$50.00	8/4
Savings	$50.00	8/5	$50.00	8/4
Groceries	$400.00	8/6	$433.00	8/5
Giving	$275.00	8/7	$275.00	8/5
Credit Card 2	$80.00	8/7	$80.00	8/5
Car Loan 1	$200.00	8/8	$200.00	8/5
Cable/Internet	$180.00	8/10	$180.00	8/5
Cell Phone	$175.00	8/11	$179.00	8/5
Sewer	$45.00	8/12	$45.00	8/5
Missionary Sponsorship	$50.00	8/15	$50.00	8/5
Auto Insurance	$80.00	8/15	$80.00	8/5
Life Insurance	$40.00	8/15	$40.00	8/5
Haircuts	$60.00	8/15	$60.00	8/5
Total Expenses	$1,835.00		$1,880.00	

Total Income	$2,190.00	$2,190.00
Total Expenses	$1,835.00	$1,880.00
Surplus*	$355.00	$310.00

Table 2

Pay Date: August 18th & 19th

	Expected Amount		Actual Amount	
Available Balance	$320.00		$310.00	
Income				
Peter's Job	$1,325.00		$1,325.00	
Mary's Job	$850.00		$850.00	
Total	**$2,495.00**		$2,485.00	

Expenses	Amount Due	Due Date	Amount Paid	Date Paid
Electric	$100.00	8/18	$114.00	8/18
Dining out	$50.00	8/19	$43.00	8/18
Water	$35.00	8/19	$35.00	8/18
Auto Fuel	$75.00	8/19	$89.00	8/18
Emergency Savings	$50.00	8/19	$40.00	8/18
Savings	$50.00	8/19	$0.00	8/18
Groceries	$400.00	8/20	$397.00	8/19
Pet Food	$40.00	8/20	$40.00	8/19
Child Care	$250.00	8/20	$250.00	8/19
Giving	$275.00	8/21	$275.00	8/19
Heat - gas	$65.00	8/21	$58.00	8/19
Medications	$35.00	8/28	$35.00	8/19
Mortgage*	$775.00	9/1	$775.00	8/19
Car Maintenance	$25.00	9/1	$25.00	8/19
Out of Pocket Medical	$40.00	9/1	$40.00	8/19
Gifts (B-day/Christmas)	$60.00	9/1	$60.00	8/19
Vacation	$100.00	9/1	$100.00	8/19
Credit Card 1	$65.00	9/1	$65.00	8/19
Total Expenses	$2,490.00			

Total Income	$2,495.00	$2,485.00
Total Expenses	$2,490.00	$2,441.00
Surplus**	$5.00	$44.00

*All or part of the Surplus from Table 1 becomes the available balance in Table 2.

*The mortgage payment could have been split between the two tables as an alternate way of covering this large expense.

**All or part of the Surplus from Table 2 becomes the available balance for next month's Table 1

As you can see, Peter and Mary's expenses were different from what they planned. This will happen. In fact, you will hardly ever have a month where everything goes as planned. That is why it is so important to be flexible and ready to make changes to your budget schedule. Higher actual expenses than what you planned for could mean saving less in a given month. Other times, higher expenses might be offset by bills that were lower than expected. Here are some ways you can handle the challenge of your expenses being higher than what you planned or your income being less than what you planned:

1. Consider exchanging a larger bill from table with a lower bill from another table.
2. Place less money in your saving account for the month.
3. If necessary, pull money from your emergency savings account. Remember to replace what you borrowed the following month(s).

ACTION STEP 4:

1. Finish your monthly budget (Steps 10-12) and budget schedule (Step 5) by filling in actual income and expense amounts and the dates they were paid. Also, complete Step 13 of the monthly budget to determine your total actual balance.

When you combine the budget with the budget schedule, you will begin to see real change come to your finances. But it must be done consistently, month after month, for lasting change to take place. Some people will only use these worksheets for one month, maybe two, and then quit. Their excuse is different but they all end up back in the same place — frustration and despair. To prevent this, follow these rules:

Rule 1 – Create a new budget every month BEFORE you get paid.

Rule 2 – Fill in the budget schedule every month BEFORE you get paid.

Rule 3 – Double check to make sure that your expenses and income are exactly the same when comparing your budget to your budget schedule.

Rule 4 – Pay your bills when you get paid. Don't wait until the bill's due date.

Rule 5 – Stick to the budget and the budget schedule throughout the month.

A budget and a budget schedule will change your finances forever. No longer will you question when a bill is due or how you will pay it. Now, your finances are organized and you are in control. Managing your finances once seemed so hard and frustrating but, with a plan, you are now on the path towards better stewardship and financial success.

Concept Review

1. Budget

Keys for Understanding

➤ A budget is born out of a desire to become a better steward of your money.

➤ A budget is a *written* plan that organizes and compares your *planned* income and expenses for the month to your *actual* income and expenses for that month.

➤ A new budget should be created every month.

➤ When you create a budget, it will be done for the next month. For example, July's budget will be created in late June.

➤ While a budget will help you know what is due and when, its limitation is in explaining how to pay for your expenses.

2. Budget Schedule

Keys for Understanding

➤ A budget schedule organizes the income and expenses listed on your budget into tables that tells you when and how to pay the bills you owe.

➤ Each table represents a paycheck you will receive in the given month. If multiple pays fall on or close to the same day, they can go into the same table.

➢ Expenses on the budget are then organized under the table in which they fit best by due date and amount. Please make sure every expense is listed in a table prior to the expense's due date. Under no circumstances should you ever pay a bill late.

➢ Some expenses may need to be split between multiple tables and paychecks because of the large amount due. Please make sure you spread the expense over tables prior to the expense's due date.

➢ Allocate the monthly surplus towards a new expense labeled "Emergency Fund."

Peter and Mary's Monthly Budget – Example

Summary	Amount
Expected Balance (Total Expected Income - Total Expected Expenses)	$25.00
Actual Balance (Total Actual Income - Total Actual Expenses)	$29.00

Income

	Income Source	Expected Amount	Pay Date 1	Pay Date 2	Pay Date 3	Pay Date 4	Table	Actual Amount
1	Peter's Job	$2,650 ($1325 per pay)	5-Aug	19-Aug			1 & 2	$2,650.00
2	Mary's Job	$1,700 ($850 per pay)	4-Aug	18-Aug			1 & 2	$1,700.00
3								
4								
5								
6								
	Total Income	$4,350.00						$4,350.00

Expenses

	Expense	Expected Amount	Due Date	Table	Actual Amount	Paid Date
1	Giving	$275.00	7th	1	$275.00	8/5
2	Giving	$275.00	21st	2	$275.00	8/19
3	Missionary Sponsorship	$50.00	15th	1	$50.00	8/5
4	Mortgage	$775.00	1st	2	$775.00	8/19
5	Groceries	$400.00	6th	1	$433.00	8/5
6	Groceries	$400.00	20th	2	$397.00	8/19
7	Dining out	$50.00	19th	2	$43.00	8/18
8	Dining out	$50.00	5th	1	$65.00	8/4
9	Water	$35.00	19th	2	$35.00	8/18
10	Sewer	$45.00	12th	1	$45.00	8/5
11	Electric	$100.00	18th	2	$114.00	8/18
12	Heat - gas	$65.00	21st	2	$58.00	8/19
13	Cell Phone	$175.00	11th	1	$179.00	8/5
14	Trash	$25.00	5th	1	$25.00	8/4
15	Car Loan 1	$200.00	8th	1	$200.00	8/5
16	Auto Fuel	$75.00	5th	1	$68.00	8/4
17	Auto Fuel	$75.00	19th	2	$89.00	8/18
18	Car Maintenance	$25.00	1st	2	$25.00	8/19
19	Auto Insurance	$80.00	15th	1	$80.00	8/5
20	Life Insurance	$40.00	15th	1	$40.00	8/5
21	Medications	$35.00	28th	2	$35.00	8/19
22	Out of Pocket Medical	$40.00	1st	2	$40.00	8/19
23	Credit Card 1	$65.00	1st	2	$65.00	8/19
24	Credit Card 2	$80.00	7th	1	$80.00	8/5
25	Haircuts	$60.00	15th	1	$60.00	8/5
26	Cable/Internet	$180.00	10th	1	$180.00	8/5
27	Gifts (B-day/Christmas)	$60.00	1st	2	$60.00	8/19
28	Vacation	$100.00	1st	2	$100.00	8/19
29	Pet Food	$40.00	20th	2	$40.00	8/19
30	Child Care	$250.00	20th	2	$250.00	8/19
31	Emergency Savings	$50.00	5th	1	$50.00	8/4
32	Emergency Savings	$50.00	19th	2	$40.00	8/18
33	Savings	$50.00	19th	2	$0.00	Did not pay
34	Savings	$50.00	5th	1	$50.00	8/4
	Total Expenses	$4,325.00			$4,321.00	

Peter and Mary's Budget Schedule - Example

Table 1					
Pay Date: August 4th & 5th					
	Expected Amount		Actual Amount		
Available Balance	$15.00		$15.00		
Income					
Peter's Job	$1,325.00		$1,325.00		
Mary's Job	$850.00		$850.00		
Total	$2,190.00		$2,190.00		
Expenses	Amount Due	Due Date	Amount Paid	Date Paid	
Dining out	$50.00	8/5	$65.00	8/4	
Trash	$25.00	8/5	$25.00	8/4	
Auto Fuel	$75.00	8/5	$68.00	8/4	
Emergency Savings	$50.00	8/5	$50.00	8/4	
Savings	$50.00	8/5	$50.00	8/4	
Groceries	$400.00	8/6	$433.00	8/5	
Giving	$275.00	8/7	$275.00	8/5	
Credit Card 2	$80.00	8/7	$80.00	8/5	
Car Loan 1	$200.00	8/8	$200.00	8/5	
Cable/Internet	$180.00	8/10	$180.00	8/5	
Cell Phone	$175.00	8/11	$179.00	8/5	
Sewer	$45.00	8/12	$45.00	8/5	
Missionary Sponsorship	$50.00	8/15	$50.00	8/5	
Auto Insurance	$80.00	8/15	$80.00	8/5	
Life Insurance	$40.00	8/15	$40.00	8/5	
Haircuts	$60.00	8/15	$60.00	8/5	
Total Expenses	$1,835.00		$1,880.00		
Total Income	$2,190.00		$2,190.00		
Total Expenses	$1,835.00		$1,880.00		
Surplus*	$355.00		$310.00		

Table 2					
Pay Date: August 18th & 19th					
	Expected Amount		Actual Amount		
Available Balance	$320.00		$310.00		
Income					
Peter's Job	$1,325.00		$1,325.00		
Mary's Job	$850.00		$850.00		
Total	$2,495.00		$2,485.00		
Expenses	Amount Due	Due Date	Amount Paid	Date Paid	
Electric	$100.00	8/18	$114.00	8/18	
Dining out	$50.00	8/19	$43.00	8/18	
Water	$35.00	8/19	$35.00	8/18	
Auto Fuel	$75.00	8/19	$89.00	8/18	
Emergency Savings	$50.00	8/19	$40.00	8/18	
Savings	$50.00	8/19	$0.00	8/18	
Groceries	$400.00	8/20	$397.00	8/19	
Pet Food	$40.00	8/20	$40.00	8/19	
Child Care	$250.00	8/20	$250.00	8/19	
Giving	$275.00	8/21	$275.00	8/19	
Heat - gas	$65.00	8/21	$58.00	8/19	
Medications	$35.00	8/28	$35.00	8/19	
Mortgage*	$775.00	9/1	$775.00	8/19	
Car Maintenance	$25.00	9/1	$25.00	8/19	
Out of Pocket Medical	$40.00	9/1	$40.00	8/19	
Gifts (B-day/Christmas)	$60.00	9/1	$60.00	8/19	
Vacation	$100.00	9/1	$100.00	8/19	
Credit Card 1	$65.00	9/1	$65.00	8/19	
Total Expenses	$2,490.00				
Total Income	$2,495.00		$2,485.00		
Total Expenses	$2,490.00		$2,441.00		
Surplus**	$5.00		$44.00		

*All or part of the Surplus from Table 1 becomes the available balance in Table 2.

*The mortgage payment could have been split between the two tables as an alternate way of covering this large expense.

**All or part of the Surplus from Table 2 becomes the available balance for next month's Table 1

Step 6:
Keeping Track of Your Finances

Goal

Learn how to use the Genesis Financial Money Tracking Worksheet to manage your daily finances.

Connection Points

1. Managing your finances on a daily basis is the best way to stay true to your budget, budget schedule, and overall financial goals.
2. Using the worksheet requires you to save receipts from things you purchase and bills you pay and log them onto the sheet daily.
3. Updating the worksheet on a daily basis requires discipline and dedication.
4. Proper use of the worksheet eliminates the guessing game of how much you have in your bank accounts or whether you paid that bill or not.

ACTION STEP 1:

1. How do you keep track of what you spend and earn every day?

_____

2. How do you know whether or not you have enough money to pay a bill that is due?

_____

3. Do you ever feel like you never know how much money you have at any given time? Why is that?

_____

    Step 6 is simple, easy to do, and can lead to big time success with your finances. At the same time, for those who skip over this step, financial doom will quickly come upon you. Now that you are paying attention, Step 6 is using the **Genesis Financial Money Tracking Worksheet** to track every penny earned and every penny spent on a daily basis. You may be asking yourself, "Isn't that what the budget and budget schedule are supposed to do?" Unfortunately, no. The budget and budget schedule organize your income and expenses, but it won't tell you when that check has cleared your bank account or when your paycheck has arrived. Keeping track of all the money coming in and going out is absolutely essential to be successful in your finances. In fact, if you do everything else perfectly, if you accomplish every one of the other steps but don't do this, you will make mistakes that will blow your budget and cause you to go backwards. Take a look at the worksheet on the next page and the instructions on page 42. Also, the Appendix has an additional copy that can be photocopied for future months.

ACTION STEP 2:

1. Begin using the Genesis Financial Money Tracking Worksheet

GENESIS MONEY TRACKING WORKSHEET

Date	Transaction Type (Deposit, Cash, Check #, Debit Card, etc.)	Description of Transaction	Payment/Debit $	Deposit/Credit $	Balance	Cleared bank account
			Starting Balance			

Here's an example of how it works:

Date	Transaction Type (Deposit, Cash, Check #, Debit Card, etc.)	Description of Transaction	Payment/Debit $	Deposit/Credit $	Balance	Cleared bank account
			Starting Balance		$123.00	
1/23	Check #304	Electric Bill	$48.00		$75.00	Cleared
1/24	Deposit	Paycheck		$625.00	$700.00	Cleared
1/25	Debit Card	Gas	$23.00		$677.00	

1. **Starting Balance** – Begin by filling in the starting balance. This would be the amount of money in your checking account (after subtracting all outstanding checks and pending purchases). Don't have a bank

account? No problem. How much cash do you have on you right now from your last paycheck? Whatever that amount is, write it in the "Starting Balance" row.

2. **Date** – Log the date of the purchase, bill or deposit in the "Date" column.

3. **Transaction Type** – List what type of transaction you made. If you received a paycheck, then write in "Deposit." If you wrote out a check to pay rent, then write in "Check" and the check number. Do that for cash, debit cards, or any other transaction type.

4. **Description of Transaction** – Describe the purchase, bill, or deposit.

5. **Payment/Debit $** – Write in the amount of the bill or purchase. This will be subtracted from the balance amount in the previous row.

6. **Deposit/Credit $** – Write in the amount of the deposit. This will be added to the balance amount in the previous row.

7. **Balance** – The "Balance" column will change depending on whether you are adding money to your account through the "Deposit/Credit" column or subtracting money through the "Payment/Debit" column.

8. **Cleared Bank Account** – Keep track of when payments and deposits hit your checking account. Do this by checking your bank account online. You should always be a step or two ahead of the bank because you are keeping track of the checking account activity in real time.

In order to make this work, you will need to fill in the worksheet every day. To do this, you will need to collect a receipt from every purchase and save it until you log that day's purchases into your Money Tracking Worksheet. You do the same for bills and deposits. Again, this must be done every day for every purchase no matter how small or insignificant the dollar amount is. This requires discipline. It needs to become as routine as brushing your teeth or eating. So, pick a time of the day when you will be able to spend fifteen minutes completing the worksheet. If you do it at night, then you will be writing in the day's transactions. If you do it in the morning, then you will likely be filling in yesterday's transactions. Whenever you do it, make sure it is done daily and you leave nothing out.

The point of this worksheet is for you to stay on top of your finances and always know how much money you have. No more guessing whether you have enough money to pay for something. Guessing leads to bounced checks and angry utility companies and landlords. Beginning can be difficult. So, start off by making a promise to yourself to fill in the worksheet every day for thirty days. What you thought would be too difficult and time-consuming will become a habit and bring unbelievable organization to your finances.

Concept Review

1.   Genesis Financial Money Tracking Worksheet

> ### *Keys for Understanding*
> ➢ Keeping your finances organized and up to date is a crucial step in becoming and staying financially successful.
> ➢ The Genesis Financial Money Tracking Worksheet will help you keep track of your daily expenses as well as your monthly income and bills, so that you always know the exact amount of money you have.

➤ The worksheet is simple and easy to use but requires discipline to update it daily.

➤ To keep the worksheet up to date, get receipts for every purchase you make in a day and record those on your worksheet the same day.

➤ Add income and monthly bills to your worksheet the same day they are received or paid.

Genesis Financial Tip:
Make It a Habit

There is a good chance you have developed some bad financial habits over the past few years. Well, now is the time to change that and perhaps one of the most important good financial habits for you to begin is tracking your finances daily through the Genesis Financial Money Tracking Worksheet. *It truly is the key to your financial success.* Eventually, the worksheet can be replaced by computer software but, for now, it will be your finances best friend. So, make it a habit to update your tracking worksheet daily and watch your success grow.

Step 7:
Open a Checking Account

Chapter Preview

Goal
Understand checking account basics and open an account for yourself.

Connection Points
1. A checking account will make it easier for you to manage your finances.
2. There are many options and features you should know before you open an account.

ACTION STEP 1:

1. Do you have a checking account or any other type of bank account? If so, where?

   _____

2. How is your income paid to you?

   _____

3. How do you pay for your bills and expenses?

   _____

4. Have you ever used a payroll cashing service? If so, how much do they charge you?

   _____

If you already have a checking account, then you can probably skip this step and move on to Step 8. If you do not have a checking account, then continue reading. Step 7 is simple — open a checking account. This step will change the way you receive your paychecks, pay bills, and manage your money. If all of that is done correctly, then it will save you time and money. Consider these things when opening an account:

- **The Bank** – The first thing you need to do is decide which bank you want to use. A good recommendation would be to use the bank where you set up your emergency savings account since they already have a relationship with you. When you go there to set up your account, it is important that you open a checking account that has no minimum balance and is completely free.

- **Direct Deposit** – It is also important that you set up your account for direct deposit. Direct deposit is where you tie your checking account to any paychecks you receive. So, instead of you receiving a paper check, the money will be transferred electronically on your pay date directly to your checking account. The money is usually (but not always) available immediately. In order to do this, you must ask your employer if direct deposit is available. If so, you typically must sign a form that includes your new checking account number and bank routing number. Both of these can be found on your new checks.

- **Checks and Debit Card** – The bank will usually give you a set of starter checks which should be a good start. Hold off on ordering any more checks unless most of your bills can only be paid by check. Ask for a debit card but decline any offer for a credit card. Debit cards can be used almost anywhere credit cards are accepted but pose less risk because they use the money that is in your bank account.

- **Overdraft Protection** – Overdraft protection allows you to spend more money than what you actually have. For example, if you spend $75 but only have $25 in your account, overdraft protection will allow the bank to cover the $50 you are short. Sounds like a good deal but beware because it will lead to financial doom. Not only do you have to pay the bank back but with additional fees of between $20 to $40 dollars. So, your $75 purchase left you negative $50 plus all the fees. To have this feature, you need a second account with your bank. This is typically a savings account. It is your choice whether you add overdraft protection, but please do not use your emergency savings account as your overdraft account. With proper budgeting and keeping a close eye on your finances through your tracking worksheet, you shouldn't be spending more than what you have.

- **Keeping track of your new checking account** – Once your account is set up, it's time to keep track of every penny that goes into the account and every penny that leaves the account. Please use the Genesis Financial Money Tracking Worksheet to do this.

- **Sign up for online access** – Online access gives you the ability to see your account over the Internet. Your account's history including cleared checks, posted debit card purchases, and deposits will appear. This is important to have because it allows you to know which transactions have posted to your bank account, which can then be cleared on your Money Tracking Worksheet. A word of caution: Please do not rely on the account balance given to you by the bank's website. It neither includes checks that have not been cashed, nor does it include debit card purchases made within 24-48 hours. That's why you use the Money Tracking Worksheet for record keeping. If you rely on the online account balance, you will certainly spend more than what you have and it will leave you in the negative.

Following these simple steps to open a checking account will save you time, money, and make your life a lot easier. No more trips to the payroll cashing store. No more fees and payday loans. No more certified checks and their fees. Step 7 may seem small but it is a giant leap forward for your finances.

Step 8:
Debt: A Simple Plan to Get Out

Chapter Preview

Goal
Learn the truth about debt and begin a systematic plan to become debt free.

Connection Points
1. The Bible is very clear about the many pitfalls and risks that come with getting into debt.
2. Getting out of debt requires patience, a sound strategy, and long term approach.
3. The Genesis Debt Priority List will help organize your debts properly.
4. Once your debts are organized, the debt snowball method will begin to eliminate your debts one by one.

Debt is not good. That is the simple truth. You must get out of debt. That is also a simple truth. In Step 8, you will begin your road towards becoming debt free. It will not happen overnight. For some, it will not even happen soon. Regardless of how much debt you have, this simple plan will provide you a way out.

For most people who have fallen behind in their finances, food and shelter get first priority while paying back debt is usually somewhere near the end of the priority list. This means that some debts may have not seen any payments towards them in a long time. That issue should have been addressed in the Genesis Financial Income and Expense Worksheet. In that worksheet, every debt should have been listed along with the minimum payment required. Because it was listed, those monthly amounts should have been added into the total expense amount. And since you needed to have a surplus at the end of the month to move on, then all of your debt's minimum payments should be currently met. However, if you did not list them and are therefore not paying them, then you must go back to Step 1 or see a Financial Coach for the **Genesis Financial Income Based Debt Repayment Plan**.

ACTION STEP 1:

1. Complete the **Genesis Debt List**

GENESIS DEBT LIST

Gather all debts you owe and complete each column. Don't leave any out. Make sure you list whether the debt has gone to a collections company. When finished, add all of your minimum monthly payments together. Do the same for the outstanding balance column.

	Company	Minimum Payment	Total Outstanding Balance	Interest Rate	In Collections?
1					
2					
3					
4					
5					
6					
7					
8					
9					
10					
11					
12					
13					
14					
15					
16					
17					
18					
19					
20					
Total:					

Add all monthly minimum payments together.

Add all outstanding balances together.

The Debt List should have everyone's name on it that you owe money. It doesn't matter if it's big or small. If you owe someone money and they haven't forgiven your debt, then you need to pay them back.

ACTION STEP 2:

1. Reorganize your debts using the **Genesis Debt Priority List**. You will organize them by placing the debt with the smallest balance in the first spot and working your way down to the largest balance in the last spot.

GENESIS DEBT PRIORITY LIST

Priority #	Company	Minimum Payment	Total Outstanding Balance	Interest Rate	In Collections?
1					
2					
3					
4					
5					
6					
7					
8					
9					
10					
11					
12					
13					
14					
15					
16					
17					
18					
19					
20					
Total:					

Add all monthly minimum payments together.   *Add all outstanding balances together.*

Step 8 is a big step. It brings back memories of past purchases of things you may not even have now. It may also bring up sad situations of divorce, illnesses, or collection notices. But with these memories come a lesson to be learned on what God thinks about debt and *Genesis Financial* believes God has a very clear picture on this subject, and it is not favorable:

- *"Just as the rich rule the poor, so the borrower is servant to the lender."* Proverbs 22:7 (NLT)
- *"Give to everyone what you owe them: Pay your taxes and government fees to those who collect them, and*

give respect and honor to those who are in authority. Owe nothing to anyone—except for your obligation to love one another..." Romans 13:7-8 (NLT)

Now that you understand what God says, there isn't much room for negotiation. Now, it's time to start paying what you owe. *But how?*

You already started the process by prioritizing which debt will be paid first — the debt with the smallest balance. But if you just paid the minimum monthly payment, it would probably take a long time to pay it off. And because you are not interested in taking a long time to pay off your debts, you need a different strategy than just paying the minimum. What you need is some extra money to throw at that debt. But where will you find the extra money? Simple. Because your emergency fund has been fully funded, you can now apply the surplus leftover at the end of every month towards the first debt. Combining the minimum payment of that first debt with the surplus will reduce the amount of time it takes to pay off that debt.

Once you have the first debt paid, it's time to give yourself a pat on the back but, you can't stop there because there is a list of people you owe money and part of being a good steward is paying them back. So, your next step is to use what many call the "debt snowball." The debt snowball is a method of paying off your debt quickly and easily using the minimum monthly payments from previous debts and applying them towards current debts. Here is an example of how it works:

Debt	Balance	Min. Payment	Surplus	Snowball Monthly Payment	
1. ABC Credit Card	$0.00	$15.00	$25.00	PAID	$15 is the minimum payment from ABC Credit Card.
					$20 is the minimum payment for the electric company.
2. Electric Company	$180.00	$20.00	$25.00	$15 + $20 + $25 = **$60**	$25 is the surplus amount.
					$60 is the total amount you pay every month.
3. Cell Phone	$235.00	$18.00	$25.00	$15 + $20 + $25 + 18 = **$78**	Once the electric company's debt is paid, use the snowball method for the cell phone debt.

As you can see, ABC Credit Card had the smallest balance so it was first on your debt priority list to pay off. You paid the minimum payment plus the surplus amount (the amount leftover at the end of the month) until the debt was paid in full. You then applied the minimum payment from ABC Credit Card with the surplus amount to the minimum payment you owe to the electric company. Now, you are paying off the debt much quicker. How much quicker? Consider this: If you just paid the minimum due to the electric company it would have taken you nine months to pay that debt off. But, by applying the snowball method and adding the previous debts minimum payment and the surplus amount, you pay off the electric company in three months!

By using the debt snowball method, you will get yourself out of debt and do it the right way. To be honest, though, it is not a quick process. Getting out of debt will always take longer than it took you to get into debt. It requires dedication to the plan and staying on budget — *every month*. I would highly recommend a Financial Coach to help with this process and encourage you along the way. They will also be able to tailor a plan for your specific situation. So, if you need help with debt, don't wait. Waiting makes it worse. Pay what you owe. That will honor God.

Concept Review

1.   Debt: What is it and how does it affect us

> **Keys for Understanding**
> ➢ Debt can come in many shapes and sizes: Credit cards, student loans, mortgages, auto loans, etc.
> ➢ When you agree to take on debt or finance something, you are promising to give a portion of your future income to get something now.
> ➢ The greatest risk you undertake by getting into debt is the uncertainty of your future income versus the certainty of repaying the debt.
> ➢ Improper planning and lack of savings are major contributors to people going into debt.

2.   Debt: God and the Bible

> **Keys for Understanding**
> ➢ God has a very clear outlook on debt and it's simple: *"Give to everyone what you owe them: Pay your taxes and government fees to those who collect them, and give respect and honor to those who are in authority. Owe nothing to anyone—except for your obligation to love one another."* Romans 13:7-8 (NLT)
> ➢ God says this because He knows, *"Just as the rich rule the poor, so the borrower is servant to the lender."* Proverbs 22:7 (NLT)
> ➢ Debt prevents us from sharing freely the money God has given us and investing in His kingdom; debt makes us slaves when Christ set us free.
> ➢ Most debt is a result of discontentment, living above one's means, and lack of prayer and faith.

3.   Debt: Debt Snowball

> **Keys for Understanding**
> ➢ The simplest and easiest way to systematically pay off debt on a monthly basis is using the debt snowball method.
> ➢ This method will pay off the debts in the order listed on the Debt Priority List.
> ➢ Up to this point, you should have been paying the minimum balance on all your debt and have reached your initial goal in funding their emergency fund (Step 4) by using the surplus after you went positive (Step 3).

➤ Now, the surplus will be added to the minimum payment on the first debt listed on your Debt Priority List. By adding to these payments together, the debt will be repaid much more quickly than just the minimum payment would achieve.

➤ Once the first debt is paid off, you will add the minimum payment from the first debt plus the surplus to the minimum payment of the second debt listed on your Debt Priority List.

➤ The process of adding the minimum payments from past debts to the surplus to the minimum payment of the current debt being paid will continue for each debt until all debt has been paid.

PART 3

THE ROAD AHEAD

"Trust in the LORD with all your heart; do not depend on your own understanding. Seek his will in all you do, and he will show you which path to take."

PROVERBS 3:4-6 (NLT)

The Road Ahead

After completing "Me, Myself, and God's Money" and "The Steps to Financial Stability," you now have a firm financial foundation to build upon. But that doesn't mean you will neither make mistakes, nor you won't be tempted to make an unwise financial decision. Those things will always be knocking on your door. You must learn how to minimize the mistakes, stay committed to the plan and control the temptations to do unwise things with your money.

This is not an easy task. There is always a "great deal" that was not included on your budget, or the unexpected bill comes in the mail that nearly wipes out the emergency fund. What about that difficult financial decision that you need to make quickly? You will need help with your finances; someone to encourage and lift you up when times are difficult and you feel like quitting; someone you can bounce ideas off of; someone who is wiser and more experienced than you. Your Financial Coach is an invaluable resource that will guide you through the financial road ahead. And, in this last part entitled "The Road Ahead," special attention will be placed on key financial topics that you and your Financial Coach should consider.

As you begin, you will notice three separate sections — "Red Lights," "Yellow Lights," and "Green Lights." Topics listed under red lights will be things you should stop doing immediately or, at least, pause for the time being until your financial situation changes. Yellow light topics will include things with which you should proceed with caution. Green light financial topics are those that you should definitely try to do even if you just start with baby steps. Please remember, though, that your Financial Coach is your best resource to personalize this information to fit your unique circumstances.

Red Lights

Red light financial topics are those that you should stop doing or temporarily stop until your financial situation clears up and becomes healthier. Please consult your Financial Coach for more specific help.

 ## Don't make any large purchases in the next six months

This may seem like an odd request but think about where you were and where you are now — pretty incredible, huh? Making a big purchase could completely undo everything you worked so hard for. Buying things like a car or house, or starting a major project will put a serious strain on your finances. It's like a man who had a heart attack leaving the hospital after recovering and immediately running a marathon. We don't need to be a doctor to realize that would be unwise and we, too, should realize that we need some time to heal financially before making major purchases. Resist the temptation. Instead, take time to get into good financial habits, make wise decisions, and bring a sense of financial peace back to your life. These are foundational steps that will prove to be priceless in your road ahead. And as you move forward, please remember that any financial peace you hope to gain through any of these steps must first begin through the peace of God.

 ## Stop spending your tax refund

It seems like, from January to April, everyone has a little more money to throw around thanks to the tax refund. For many people, it is the largest one-time paycheck they will receive all year. So, what should you do with all that money? Consider these four things the next time you receive your tax refund:

1. *Fund your emergency savings account* – Why not consider using part of your refund to build your emergency fund? You'll thank yourself when the unexpected comes up. See Step 4 in "Steps to Financial Stability" for more information.
2. *Pay off the debt on your Debt Priority List* – Okay, so this isn't the most fun use of your tax refund but consider how happy you will be when you can say that you are debt free. Not many people can say that these days. Simply add up the outstanding balances from your remaining debts listed on your debt priority list and see how many your refund can pay off.
3. *Save* – If you have funded your emergency account and paid off your debts, then why not save the tax refund? You have goals and dreams that probably require money, so why not begin saving to turn your goals and dreams into reality?
4. *Get your refund directly deposited into your checking account* – If a company is filing your taxes for you,

chances are they will offer to have your refund sent to a prepaid card or gift card — don't do this. You will end up spending it on junk food and a new TV. Just have it sent directly to your checking account and avoid wasting this once-a-year opportunity.

5. *Resist the Refund Anticipation Loans/Checks* – Tax preparation companies love giving you your tax refund immediately. They call these instant refunds "anticipation loans" or "anticipation checks." The funny thing is that, they don't do this for free. They charge you fees or a percentage of your refund for being able to get the refund right away. That means you get less money because you are impatient. Don't do this. If you followed steps outlined earlier, you will not need the money in the next thirty seconds. Wait for one to two weeks and get your full refund and get it directly deposited into your checking account.

Stop using check cashing and payday loan services

Payday loans are short-term loans with extremely high interest rates. You essentially borrow money from your next paycheck and pay a percentage or flat dollar amount or fee to the company giving you the loan. Sounds convenient, right? Not really when you are considering what the fees can be. Take a look at this example: You loan $300 from a payday loan company with a loan fee of $25 for every $100 borrowed (a typical fee charged by these companies). In two weeks, you must pay them back the full $300 plus the $25 for every $100 borrowed. That means you will owe the payday loan company $375 ($300 + $75). If you think about the annual percentage rate on this loan it would equate to 650% Annual Percentage Rate (APR). Would you ever borrow money to buy a car or house at 650% interest? Of course not. Then why borrow next week's paycheck at 650% APR? Follow the steps outlined in "Steps to Financial Stability" and you will never have to use one of these services.

Don't shop at rent-to-own stores

When you need an appliance or some other household good, rent-to-own stores provide a popular way of purchasing these items. Beware of the low weekly or monthly rates they charge you because they often come with interest rates between 30-60% APR. So, when you finally pay off the item you rented, you actually paid hundreds more than what it costs in a traditional store. Consider this example: A new TV will cost $2,183 at a traditional store. The same TV at a rent-to-own store has the same sticker price on it but comes with a convenient weekly payment option. Instead of paying the full $2,183 immediately, you can take home the TV for $34.99 per week for 104 weeks. Do the math and you will find that this TV will cost you $3,638.96 ($34.99 × 104 weeks). This is $1,455.96 ($3,638.96 - $2,183) more than what you would have paid if you paid cash. The best alternative for items you need with a limited budget is to find a used appliance store. They offer are a fraction of the cost of new items and save you weekly payments and high interest.

Don't take an expensive vacation

As you begin to see your finances take a turn for the better, there is a funny thing that begins to happen. You begin to start thinking about all the things you once thought were never possible. And as you see your savings account grow, one of the first things you may want to do is get away and take a vacation. After all, you've earned it, *right*?

As harmless as it may seem and as much as it may be needed, I encourage you to wait. This is one of those red lights that doesn't mean *never*, but rather just not right now. Resist the temptation to take this vacation even if it is not "that expensive." Too many have done this either as a stress relief or in celebration and have found themselves blowing their savings account and using credit cards. One simple trip can turn into months of financial recovery. A time will come when this dream of taking a vacation will not just become a reality but also become a financial reality. Consider setting up a vacation account at your bank and saving money towards an annual vacation. This will hopefully offset the majority if not all of the vacation's cost. Be patient and wait. You will thank yourself for it later.

Don't take on any additional debt

Do you want to know how you are doing better financially? The answer is in your mailbox and inbox. What do I mean? Simple. As you begin to pay off your debt, other debt companies take notice and see that you are becoming an attractive customer for whatever they are trying to sell you, in this case, more debt. So, you'll see one preapproval letter after another start pouring in. You have suddenly become popular!

Don't fall for this. People don't have debt collectors calling after them and filing for bankruptcy because they are debt free and doing well financially. There is a reason God says stay away from debt. He knows that debt binds you to the credit company. And when we do that we give up little pieces of freedom that Jesus purchased for us.

Stay clear of taking on any additional debt. Learn how to live without the world's answer to buying the things they can't afford. Live simpler with less stuff and I guarantee you that you won't miss it.

To aid in this process, consider opting out of the many credit card and other debt offerings that flood your mail box and inbox. You can opt out of these mailings by calling toll-free 1-888-5-OPT-OUT (1-888-567-8688) or visit www.optoutprescreen.com. The phone number and website are operated by the major consumer reporting companies.

However, you may counter this argument with how getting a new credit card would help you rebuild your credit. After all, you are more responsible now and won't make the same mistakes again. Please remember that your credit score is nothing more than the world's grading system for debt. It's how the world knows whether you use debt well or not. Think about that for a second. The world is grading you on how well you use something that God says not to use. As much as I would recommend the majority of people completing *Genesis Financial* to stay clear of debt at any level, I realize that some may still go forward with things like credit cards. So, if this is you, then go to the next section and see how to proceed with great caution with a credit card.

Yellow Lights

Yellow light financial topics are those that should be treated with great caution and only entered into with careful planning. Please consult your Financial Coach for more specific help.

Be very careful about getting any credit cards

If you are reading this section without reading what I said in "Red Lights" about not getting into any additional debts, then please go back and read that first. If you have read it and still want to continue then please listen carefully to a few suggestions on how to use credit cards wisely:

1. *Choose the card and limit wisely* – Make sure you pick a card with low fees and gives generous benefits for being a customer. However, the most important thing you can do initially is to set your credit limit at a low ceiling, something like $500. This will help prevent digging yourself into too far of a hole if you suddenly become financially irresponsible.

2. *Use your credit card for small but essential purchases* – How you use a credit card can be one of the greatest factors in your ability to pay back what you temporarily borrowed. Stay with me here: If you use your credit card for things you would normally buy like gas, your cell phone bill, or groceries, then you are spending money that is already a part of your budget. However, using you credit card for something like fast food or that new drink at the coffee shop is probably not a part of your budget, which means you have no plan of how to pay for it when the bill becomes due. Therefore, use your credit card for smaller bills and expenses that are on your budget regularly.

3. *Regularly account for the money you spend on your credit card* – It's so easy to use a credit card because it doesn't reduce the amount available in your checking account. But what if it did? What if you accounted for your credit card purchases just as if it was coming out of your checking account? This is a simple and easy step in managing your credit card so that you don't have to figure out how to pay off the balance when the bill is due. Simply place your credit card on your Genesis Financial Money Tracking Worksheet and continually add the purchases you make to its balance. Then, subtract the new balance from the credit card from the total outstanding balance. While this money didn't actually come out of your checking account, it will show as if it did on your tracking worksheet. Then, when your credit card bill is due, you will have that money in your checking account to pay the bill.

4. *Pay your total balance off every month* – This should be a no-brainer. If you followed the previous three steps then you should be able to pay your bill off every month.

Getting into any financial contract

How many one or two year contracts have you entered into and regretted? There is a reason contracts exist. Companies know that whatever they are offering you will always be more appealing in the beginning than in the end. You are more willing to enter into a contract for something new or shiny than something used and beat up. This means you are okay with paying for that new thing based on the terms of the contract. But, as time goes on and something new and better comes out, your feelings quickly fade for what you have. But you can't do anything about it because you are legally obligated to fulfill your end of the contract, which means paying off the balance of what you owe or completing your time obligation.

Getting into any financial contract is a serious business even if it is just with the cable company. Simply ask what the penalty is for breaking the contract and you'll realize how serious they are and their willingness to take you to collections to get it. Are you willing to take the risk that comes with it? Be careful. Contracts bind you in much the same way as debt. Seek advice from your Financial Coach before entering into any financial contracts.

 ## Loaning money

So your friend needs money and sees how well you are now doing, so your friend comes and asks for a small loan. What do you do? This is one of the most difficult situations you can find yourself in. Before, you wouldn't have had the money to loan but now you do. You know that and so does your friend. So, if you say no, then you are afraid that it will affect you friendship. If you decide to loan the money, then my best advice to you is:

1. *Make sure it is a legitimate need* – Don't loan money to your friend so they can go out to dinner or buy a new TV. You know the difference between needs and wants, so make sure it is going towards a need.
2. *Give it. Don't loan it.* – Loan the money as a gift. In other words, give it your friend with no expectation of them being able to pay it back. Don't tell them that but just expect that they won't pay it back. That way, you gave towards a need to help your friend and, if they choose to pay you back, then its all the better. But if they don't, your friendship won't suffer.

 ## Be cautious with the little things

Too many financial problems start with the seemingly small and insignificant purchases — the coffee shop drink you need regularly, the special Friday lunch out, the unnecessary things purchased but not on your grocery list. The "little things" are different for everyone but everyone has those little things and it's those things that can devastate a budget. Why? For some reason, anything under $10 doesn't seem like anything to us, as if those things don't add up by month's end. The problem is they do add up and often more than what we ever notice. They are hidden from us because we often put them on our credit card and forget about it until the bill is due. Those small things get lost amongst all the bigger things and we tend to trivialize them. Don't do this. Be careful with the little things and know that little things become big things and big things can turn you upside down financially.

Green Lights

Green light financial topics are those that you should do without hesitation. As always, consult your Financial Coach for specific help.

Give as generously as your budget allows

The Bible says in 2 Corinthians 9:7 (NASB) "*… for God loves a cheerful giver.*" Other verses and stories throughout the Bible point to God's desire for Christians to be generous with their finances and give towards the needs that surround us. You may have never even thought about giving in the past because you simply had nothing to give. Or, you may have wanted to give and were only able to give a small amount, less than what you really wanted.

Giving of your finances is not something anyone can tell you to do. It needs to originate in your heart as an expression of your love and worship for God and your love of others. It's hard to explain the pull that occurs when you feel drawn to a particular need that causes you to want to give financially. It may be giving regularly to your church, a specific missionary or a missions organization. Wherever you heart is drawn, give freely — don't let anyone force you to give somewhere or a certain amount. That's what Paul meant in 2 Corinthians 9:7 with the word "cheerfully."

> *Let your budget begin to reflect the pull of your heart.*

Let your budget begin to reflect the pull of your heart. If you desire to give financially, then begin scheduling it in your budget. Adjustments may need to be made elsewhere but, if it is a desire of your heart, the sacrifice will come easily. And when you give, give generously. Giving in general should reflect what we have been given. So, think of all the things God has given you and when you can't think of any more, think of the cross. God's generous giving to us has been and will always be matchless. This should compel us to not only be cheerful with our gifts but also generous.

Begin saving money up to your emergency fund goal

You should have some money saved in your emergency savings account. After all, that was Step 4 in "Steps to Financial Stability." But is the amount you have enough to cover a real financial emergency?

If you ask financial professionals about the amount you should save in your emergency fund you will undoubtedly get different answers. Some say three months of living expenses while others will increase that to six months or even as much as a year. Doing this sounds wise and prudent until you actually calculate that number and compare it to what you currently have saved. For example, if you calculate your living expenses over the next three months to be around $12,000 and you begin saving $50 a month in your emergency fund to reach that $12,000 goal, it would take you twenty years to reach that amount. Add in the fact that you are probably saving money in a bank account, which is paying you no interest, and you will probably begin to scratch your head at some point questioning whether this was ever a good idea.

Here is an alternative. Your emergency fund is for financial emergencies. So, think about all the financial emergencies that could occur. Something could happen to your car — an accident or mechanical failure. Something could happen to you — a broken leg or unemployment. Something could happen to your house — a pipe that bursts or a refrigerator that dies. How do we calculate a realistic number to set as your emergency fund savings goal?

Determine the amount you are actually at risk. What I mean is that you probably have insurance to cover your car, health, and house. Find out what your deductibles are for each and add them together (*this may be a good time to calculate the cost of switching to a lower deductibles which reduces the amount you need to save — don't worry, it won't increase your insurance premiums as much as you think*). Next, add in another $500 to $1,000 for the mechanical failures to your car and house. Then add two months of living expenses which would be the total expected expense amount from your last two month's budgets. Once you have added all those figures together, you now have a realistic emergency fund savings goal. It may seem large at first compared to what you are saving, but remember to use large chunks of money like an income tax refund to help get there quicker. You'll reach your goal before you know it!

🚦 Meet with a financial professional to discuss establishing retirement plans

Thinking about your financial future is important. Beginning to plan for it is even more important. My guess is that while you knew retirement planning was important, it was no way even close to being on your radar. Well, now it should be.

It's time to take retirement planning seriously even if you never plan on retiring fully. So, talk to your pastor, trusted friend, or Financial Coach about someone who could help in this area. There are many things to consider — too many to discuss in this course. Find a Christian financial advisor and get a plan started that puts you on a path to saving for retirement.

🚦 Combine your finances if you are married

If you are married then you need to have a joint bank account. No excuses and no good reasons to the contrary will do. God says that when a man and woman come together in marriage, they are ONE. That means your bank accounts should be ONE. Separate bank accounts will lead to separate financial decisions. Separate financial decisions lead you to say things to your spouse like, "My money…" and "Your money…." This will lead to secrets, dishonesty, and hiding money. Before you know it, you are living separate lives. At that point, the only thing you share in common is the occasional meal together and a last name. If you allow it, money will drive a wedge in your marriage unless you and your spouse take a stand and say, "No more!" Do these things:

- Bring all bank accounts under both names.
- Work together every month on the finances.
- Together, follow the steps in "Steps to Financial Stability."
- Create financial goals together.

- Hold each other accountable to the goals and plans you made.
- Pray together. Ask that God would bring your hearts and minds together on financial issues and give you wisdom to make the right decisions.
- Meet with a Financial Coach together.

You are in this together. Commit yourself spiritually, physically, and financially to one another and your marriage will become inseparable.

 ## Set financial goals for yourself or your family

Setting financial goals is often the first step many will complete when beginning any type of comprehensive financial planning. But if I asked you to do this a few months ago your answer to this would probably have been *"To make it month's end without running out of money."* Financial goals were a pipe dream a few months ago. It's not that you didn't have them but that you just didn't see any realistic way of making any of them come true. Well, today is a different story.

It's time to begin putting your financial goals for you and your family on paper and making a realistic plan to achieve them. Your Financial Coach will help you with this process. Remember, make sure each goal is realistic, prudent, and achievable. Saying that you want a beach house with a boat in ten years and only saving $50 a month to get there is unrealistic, unwise, and unachievable. Be smart and plan wisely.

 ## Be Patient with yourself

Patience is a lost art. In a "gotta have it now" type of world, there are many wrong ways to do something to get what you want but usually only one right way. That right way will typically require waiting and being patient. Patience is something people don't value much anymore because we have found so many ways around it. Credit cards and loans allow people to forgo patiently saving and get what they want now. At what cost, though? Have you ever considered the cost of impatience? Probably not initially because instant gratification blinds the person who is impatient. But when the blindfold is taken off and the payments and interest live longer than the item we so desperately wanted years ago, the true cost of impatience is realized. Patience honors God and it saves you from making unwise decisions. Save for a purchase rather than use a credit card. Refrain from loans. The best financial decisions you can make will be ones that are well thought out and reviewed by someone wiser than you, like your Financial Coach. Go slow and take your time because patience requires discipline and commitment and these will lead to good stewardship.

Final Thoughts

Completing the Genesis Financial Workbook is a big financial step in the right direction. I know it wasn't easy. It really did take dedication, discipline, determination and desperation. But you did it and I am proud of you. You will probably be quick to admit that God did some amazing things through this process. Remember who your God is and don't lose faith when things get hard.

I will say though, the end of this journey can spell troubled waters ahead. Some are quick to forget the things they learned in the workbook and let the old financial habits come back into their life. Don't do that! Stick to the plan, keep track of your finances daily and meet with your Financial Coach every month. This will keep your eyes focused and your feet moving forward on the right pathway towards your financial goals.

But, we need your help.

Up to this point, you have not been asked to pay anything for the services you have received. However, what we do is not free. Many hours are spent meeting with people that face similar circumstances you once did. The costs associated with Genesis Financial are covered through regular financial support from people who partner with us on a monthly basis.

You learned the importance of giving and being generous. Now it's time to put it in action.

Please stand with us and give towards the next student.

If you found value in the program you just completed, and find yourself in a better financial spot now compared to when you began, I simply ask that you would consider a regular monthly donation to cover the costs for the *next* student who takes this class. Pass the blessing on. Without the support from someone before you, the financial help you just received might not have been available. I invite you to go to our website www.alphastrategies.org and click on the Donate tab.

Genesis Financial is a ministry of Alpha Strategies Group, a non-profit organization. Alpha Strategies Group is a collaboration of Christ centered financial ministries whose focus is to provide biblical financial counsel, clearly teach God's word on proper financial management and provide consulting services to churches and organizations.

APPENDIX

GENESIS FINANCIAL MONEY TRACKING WORKSHEET

Date	Transaction Type (Deposit, Cash, Check #, Debit Card, etc.)	Description of Transaction	Payment/Debit $	Deposit/Credit $	Balance	Cleared bank account
			Starting Balance			

Genesis Financial Budget Worksheet

Summary	Amount
Expected Balance (Total Expected Income - Total Expected Expenses)	
Actual Balance (Total Actual Income - Total Actual Expenses)	

Income							
Income Source	Expected Amount	Pay Date 1	Pay Date 2	Pay Date 3	Pay Date 4	Table	Actual Amount
1							
2							
3							
4							
5							
6							
Total Income							

Expenses					
Expense	Expected Amount	Due Date	Table	Actual Amount	Paid Date
1					
2					
3					
4					
5					
6					
7					
8					
9					
10					
11					
12					
13					
14					
15					
16					
17					
18					
19					
20					
21					
22					
23					
24					
25					
26					
27					
28					
29					
30					
31					
32					
Total Expenses					

GENESIS FINANCIAL BUDGET SCHEDULE

Table 1

Pay Date _____

	Amount			
Available Balance				
Income				
Total				

Expenses	Amount Due	Due Date	Amount Paid	Date Paid
Total Expenses				

Total Income				
Total Expenses				
Surplus				

Table 2

Pay Date _____

	Amount			
Available Balance				
Income				
Total				

Expenses	Amount Due	Due Date	Amount Paid	Date Paid
Total Expenses				

Total Income				
Total Expenses				
Surplus				

Table 3

Pay Date _____

	Amount			
Available Balance				
Income				
Total				

Expenses	Amount Due	Due Date	Amount Paid	Date Paid
Total Expenses				

Total Income				
Total Expenses				
Surplus				

Table 4

Pay Date _____

	Amount			
Available Balance				
Income				
Total				

Expenses	Amount Due	Due Date	Amount Paid	Date Paid
Total Expenses				

Total Income				
Total Expenses				
Surplus				

Notes:

Additional Resources from
Alpha Strategies Group

www.alphastrategies.org

Teaching the church ... **Kingdom Crossroads**

Kingdom Crossroads is a ministry designed to **reveal** the Father's heart on finances, **teach** the church a life changing financial plan and **release** believers into their purpose. This approach is like a triple braided cord that weaves together three separate classes into one dynamic class offered through:

- Classes
- Small Group Study
- Weekend Workshops

Complete with its own book and study guide, the course is designed for Christians who already have a general knowledge of how to handle money but desire to go deeper in order to remove the financial barriers that often prevent people from realizing the gifts and living out their purpose.

Chad's Blog ... **Financial PathWays**

Subscribe to Chad's blog where all sorts of financial topics are discussed. They will challenge and encourage you to keep Christ as the center of your money and financial decisions.

Additional Material and Worksheets

Need additional materials and worksheets? There are many materials and worksheets from Genesis Financial and Kingdom Crossroads available online at www.alphastrategies.org. In addition, you can buy Chad's latest books and workbooks.